FREEDOM
The Liberty that Repentance Brings

FREEDOM
The Liberty that Repentance Brings

An Investigation of True Repentance
by Ed Marr

Christian Literature & Artwork
A BOLD TRUTH Publication

Dedication

I thank my Heavenly Father, for His grace which, as a spiritual endowment, enabled me to fulfill His charge to me to write this investigation.

Unless otherwise indicated, Bible quotations are taken from the King James Version of the Bible. Copyright © 1988 by B. B. Kirkbride Bible Company, Inc.,

Thompson-Chain Reference Bible, 5th Improved Edition. Also, from the Amplified Bible. Copyright © 1987 by The Zondervan Corporation and the Lockman Foundation

The Strong's Exhaustive Concordance of the Bible. Copyright © 1990 by Thomas Nelson Publishers.

1st Printing
Volume One Repentance:
The Doctrine of God and The Knowledge of Salvation
Copyright © 2004 by Ed Marr
ISBN 1-594675-59-7

2nd Printing w/New Title and Revisions
FREEDOM - The Liberty that Repentance Brings
Copyright © 2014 by Ed Marr
ISBN 13: 978-0-9904376-8-0

Printed in the United States of America

Bold Truth Publishing
300 West 41st
Sand Springs, Oklahoma 74063
www.BoldTruthPublishing.com

All rights reserved solely by the author. The author guarantees all contents are original and do not infringe upon the legal rights of any other person or work. No part of this book may be reproduced in any form without the permission of the author.

The views expressed in this book are not necessarily those of the publisher.

Volume 1
Table of Contents

Author's Preface .... *i*
Introduction: The Birth of a Concept. 1

BOOK 1
Chapter 1: Theological Concepts and Ideas 5
   Man's Traditional Precepts 8
   A Limited Grace Period is not an Age of Grace 12
   The Age of Grace or the Age of Promiscuity 14
   A Topical Investigation of Grace 15
   The Nomenclature of Grace 16
   Grace Applications 16
   Contrast to/of Grace 21
   Itemized Bipolarities of Grace 21
   Church Distinctions 26
   An Implanted Heart is a Saved Soul 27
   Heaven's Court 31
   Carnal Attitudes and Hostile Mind Sets 33
   The Elements of Criminal and Civil Law 34
   Iniquity is to a Guilty Mind 35
   The Seventh Day 36
   The Prophetic Word of Faith 40
   There's a Warrant Out for Your Arrest! 42
   The Call of Repentance 43
   An Elementary Presumption 44
   The Presumptive Heritage of the Church 45
   Doing Time with 3 Hots and a Cot 48
   A Prisoner of Jesus Christ 49

Chapter 2: Repentance In the Book of Genesis..........................51
   He Shall Sever and His Wrath Shall Fall 51
   God Shall Set His Face Against the Crookedness of Man........55
   The Evidence Speaks for Itself 56
   Did God?..58
   We Must Regret Our Evil Activity 58
   A Lemon is not a Make of an Automobile 61
   Noah Found Grace 62
   One Choice is No Choice..62
   Repentance as a Memorial..63

Chapter 3: Repentance In the Book of Exodus 65
   Freedom from Bondage 65
   The Violent Take it by Force...66
   Repentance at the Tabernacle..67
   A Tabernacle, Temple or a Shrine...68
   Types and Shadows...69
   Repentance as the Knowledge of Salvation............................69
   The Urim and Thummin 71
   Long Standing Disobedience 72
   False Repentance 74
   Turning State's Evidence 74
   We Must Repent of all Our Evils..75
   Repentance is What We Must Do, Ahead of Time 77
   The Reward of Iniquity or the Recompense of the Reward......78
   Withdraw or Withdrawals 80
   The Untouchables 81

Chapter 4: Repentance In the Book of Leviticus 83
   Carnal Knowledge is the Knowledge of Salvation 83
   The Head of the Bull is Cattle-Mindedness...........................87
   A Law Abiding Citizen..88
   Repentance is the Affliction of The Soul................................89
   The Law of Leprosy...90
   Leprous America..91
   Weapons of Mass Destruction 91

A Day to Atone and a Day of Salvation 92
To Appease the Gods 94
Fodder for the Gods 95
The Law of Repentance 96
To Please Almighty God.. 97
Our Atonement is Our Involvement............................... 98
The "House of Replies" 99
A Cell Within a Box 100

Chapter 5: Repentance In the Book of Numbers 103
To Bear the Iniquity 103
The Smoking Gun/Relic 103
Leadership as a Barometer..................................... 105
Keep the Charge... 106
A Now Word of Faith is not to be Repented of 107
Meat in God's House 108

Chapter 6: Repentance In the Book of Deuteronomy..... 109
Repentance, Even in the Latter Days........................... 109
To Remain Impenitent is to Remain Ignorant of Our Future... 110
Repentance Will Cause God to Rejoice Over Us for the Good.. 110
Carnality as Dung/Putting on the Dog.......................... 111
The Dung Smear 112
Carnality, the Land Mines of the Soul 113
Mind Your Own Business 114
A Shovel Among Your Weapons 115
God Does Not Want to Step in It 116
Times of War Should be Times of Reformation 117
Repentance as a Tool of the Trade 117
The Proverb of the Shovel 118
The Shovel Known as Repentance................................ 118
The Reason and the Purpose.................................... 119
Before the Well, There was the Shovel......................... 120

Chapter 7: Repentance In the Book of Joshua 121
- Impressions of Deception 121
- Finally, Somebody Caught the Revelation....................122
- Something Sinister..123
- The A'chan Factor and the Accursed Thing 124

Chapter 8: Repentance In the Book of Judges 125
- To Judge is to Self Examine......................................125
- I Don't Know!..126
- A Crisis Intervention Technique 127

Chapter 9: Repentance In the Book of Ruth 129
- Origin of Incest 129
- Carnal Progeny 129
- The Caste System 130
- Repentance Given to the Gentiles 131
- A Method of Operation 132
- Progeny Means Fruit 133
- The Progeny of Repentance 133

Chapter 10: Repentance In the Book of 1st Samuel 135
- The Mantle of Repentance..135
- The Oil and the Wine 136
- The Iniquity of Stubbornness....................................137
- The "Yada, Yada, Yada," of "Yea But" 138
- Legal Claims 140
- Illustrated "Buts" 141

Chapter 11: Repentance In The Book of 2nd Samuel............145
- Repentance Must Cost Something 145
- Truth or Consequences 145
- Foolishness is Carnality 146
- The Catered Heart 147

Chapter 12: Repentance In The Book of 1st Kings 149
- In League with Our Lobbyist 149

Presumption Negates Repentance 150

Chapter 13: Repentance In the Book of 2nd Kings 151
Talk About Going to Hell in a Handbasket 151
The Church that is Defined by Faith and Repentance 152
The Line of Righteous Judgment 152
Repentance Brings Restoration 153

BOOK 2
Chapter 14: Repentance In the Book of 1st Chronicles
The Cities of Refuge
Our Kinsman Redeemer
The Altar as Asylum Vs the Altar of Asylum
The Cities of Refuge were not Permanent Abodes
From Carnality to Spiritual Maturity
Jurisdiction
The Skirts of the Vatican
The Six Cities of Refuge
A Circus Act
The Clandestine Operation of Carnality

Chapter 15: Repentance In the Book of 2nd Chronicles
Name Your Criteria 174
A Lifestyle of Repentance is a Solemn Covenant with Almighty God
Repentance is that which We Do for Others
Repentance as a Rod of Correction
Age Has Nothing to do with It, but Repentance Does

Chapter 16: Repentance In The Book of Ezra
A Ready Scribe in the Land of Persia (Iraq/Iran)
Appointed is Different from Chosen

Chapter 17: Repentance In The Book of Nehemiah
A Man at the Right Place for the Right Time
These Walls Had to be Maintained

Chapter 18: Rep entance In The Book of Esther
    Intercourse in the Inner Court

Chapter 19: Repentance In the Book of Job
    The Abominations of Carnality
    Habeas Corpus is a Demand to Bring that Man to Court
    Making Amends for Carnality
    I Abhor Myself in Dust and Ashes

Chapter 20: Repentance In the Book of Psalms
    The Law of Repentance
    Opening Arguments: A Previously Documented Homicide Case
    The Charges of the Accused
    Trial Proceedings & Court Stipulations
    Stipulation 1: Specific Mercy for Specific Sin
    Stipulation 2: David Shouldered His Guilt and Shame
    The Ma' shak and the Ma' lach
    Conviction is a Useful Tool
    Circumstances Involved & the Ramifications It Caused
    Stipulation 3: Sin Victimizes God
    Stipulation 4: Carnality Must Be Acknowledged
    Stipulation 5: God is All Knowing
    A Psychological Profile
    The Four Quadrants of Self
    Stipulation 6: Honoring the Faith Contract
    Stipulation 7: Repentance Thwarts the Difficulties of Life
    Stipulation 8: Carnal Satisfaction or Spiritual Sanctification
    Stipulation 8a: A Case for Amnesty
    Stipulation 9: O God! Retool My Life
    Stipulation 9a: Quid Pro Quo
    R & R
    Stipulation 10: Which Cast Are You Talking About?
    Repentance That Should be Suspect

Stipulation 11: The Freedom of a Liberated Heart
    Stipulation 11a: Salvation's Nomenclature
Stipulation 12: The Defense of a Liberated Heart
Stipulation 13: Practical Instruction Begets Practical Faith
Stipulation 14: Blood Guiltiness
Salvation is Never to be Neglected
    Stipulation 14a: The Tongue of Righteousness
Stipulation 15: Repentance Must Never be Ignored or Neglected
    Stipulation 15a: Sacrifices of the Heart
    Stipulation 15b: Make a Joyful Noise
A Thorn in the Flesh
Closing Arguments: To Build the Spiritual Walls of Righteousness
Elements of the Law of Repentance

Chapter 21: Repentance in the Book of Proverbs
    The First Principle of Repentance
    Faith and Repentance Go Hand in Hand
    The Difference Between an Argument and a Debate
    What is Righteousness?
    Scriptural Examples of the Righteousness of God
    Righteousness Must be Sought After
    Righteousness Must be Taught
    The Influence of Righteousness
    The Purpose of God's Righteousness
    The Duplicity of Judgment
    Three Natures
    The Purpose and Reason of and for Righteousness
    The Stampede of the Righteous
    The Fruit of Righteousness
    The Sacrifices of Righteousness
    How does God Reveal His Righteousness?
    The Standard of Righteousness is the Flag of Faith
    The Insignia of Righteousness
    The Guidon

    Righteousness as a Drill Instructor
    Hop-A-Long, Skip-A-Long Carnality

Chapter 22: Repentance In the Book of Ecclesiastes
    It's All About Carnality!
    No Righteous Judgment, No Execution
    Moved With Envy
    The Subject of the Sons of Men
    We Must Be Smarter than the Equipment
    Carnal Bestiality
    Man's Probation is a Time of Conformity to a Godly Moral Obligation
    The Possibility of Conformity
    Just What Are you Doing?
    The Whole Duty of Man
    That Which is Deep is Known by He Who is Deeper Still

Chapter 23: Repentance In the Book of Isaiah
    Sin is a Voluntary Transgression of the Moral Law
    What is Voluntariness?
    Selfishness: The Deifying of Self
    Come Now, Let Us Reason Together
    The Condition of "If"
    Woe is Me! I am Undone!
    The Parasite of the Soul
    The Kiln of Righteousness
    The Furnace of Repentance
    A Man of Unclean Lips
    The Call in that Day
    Carnality Shall Not be Purged Until the Day You Die
    Flopping About on a Dry Dock
    Double for Your Trouble
    Wake Up Thou Sluggard!
    A Bargain with Death
    A Day of Trouble and the Day of Salvation

Baring It All Means to Come Clean
Ghost Towns, Abandoned Buildings and Waste Land
Wicked Ways and Premeditated, Unrighteous Thoughts
Ulterior Motives of Predetermined, Carnal Mind Sets
The Stuff of Fairy Tales
The Book of Rebellion

Chapter 24: Repentance In the Book of Jeremiah
The Face of an Effeminate Man
A Method of Application
Solomon's Chariot
Playing the Harlot with Many Lovers
Self Exaltation
The Topography of Man's Carnality
Who Are You in League With?
Petra: A Physical Parallel of a Spiritual Truth
From a Prison to a Prism
Self Absorbed in Their Own Self Centeredness
There is No Shame!
Religious Overtones and Sanctimonious Mind Sets
A Strong Indictment to the Ungodly for Righteousness
Coddled and Justified Carnality
Birds of Ill Omen
That Thou Mayest be Saved
The Copulation of Carnality
God Alone Reserves the Right to Reverse
The Heart of the Matter is Man's Character
Infidelity is Apostasy
What is Apostasy?
The Dry, Hot Wind of Judgment
His Horses are Swifter than Eagles
The Travail of the Soul
Till the Fallow Ground
Getting Bloody in the Spirit
An Imperfection to the Vessel
The Finger Prints of Carnality

Self Torment is to Be a Terror to Thy Carnal Self
and to Thy Carnal Friends
God's Promises are not Different from His Commands
Amend Your Ways

Chapter 25: Repentance In The Book of Lamentations
That Which Is Better
How Could This Happen?
What is Selfishness?
The School of Selfishness
Characteristics of Selfishness
A National Funeral
The Birthing of Righteous Judgment
Substance Must Precede Evidence
The Measure of Faith and the Measuring Line
of Judgment

Chapter 26: Repentance In the Book of Ezekiel
Weapons of Judgment
The Pen is Mightier than the Sword
Every Tongue that Shall Rise Against Thee in Judgment
To Judge Means to Endure
Wickedness in the Sanctuary
A Mitigation of Judgment
Repent and Turn Away From Your Idols
Carnality Shall Be Our Ruin
Errant Proverbs
The Difference Between a Confession and a
Profession
A Man's Lifestyle and His Name Are Equally
The Same
Observations Are Not Judgment Calls
Repentance is Essential to Purity and Righteousness
The Death of the Wicked
The Death of the Saints
The Wickedness of the Wicked

The Way of the Lord is not Equal

Chapter 27: Repentance In the Book of Daniel
The Unencumbered Soul
Show The Reality of Your Repentance
Animal Impulses and Carnal Tendencies
Liberate Yourself From Your Iniquitous Thoughts
Man's Carnality is the Scent Which the Dogs of Hell Follow
The Dogs of Hell

BOOK 3
Chapter 28: Repentance In the Book of Hosea
The Very First
Spiritual Adultery
The Progenitive Qualities of Repentance
A Journey to Self Recovery
To Judge Yourself Unworthy of Eternal Life
The Golden Rule of Obligation

Chapter 29: Repentance In the Book of Joel
The Rules of Engagement Have Changed
Awake to Repentance
Rend Your Heart and not Your "holy" Garments
Torn "holy" Garments
Cross Dressers and Switch Hitters Are an Abomination
Shearing Stress of Carnality
Another Man's Scruples
Binding and Loosing
Create a Faith Environment for God to Move

Chapter 30: Repentance In the Book of Amos
Establish Judgments at the Gates
Repentance Postpones God's Judgment
To Seek Means to Activate Litigation
Navy S.E.A.L. (Sea, Air and Land)

The Treader of Grapes and the Winepress of God
Portraits of Travail
The Identity of the Seal
Repentance as a "Stay of Execution
Final Appeals for a "Stay of Execution
Only Those on Death Row Know
Prisonization and Institutionalization
The Absence of Righteous Judgment
Workers of Righteousness

Chapter 31: Repentance In the Book of Obediah
Just Who Was Esau, Anyway?
An Underlying Current
A Lifestyle of Carnality
What's in Your Wallet?
Respect Your Inheritance
The Elder to Serve the Younger
A Savior to Judge

Chapter 32: Repentance In the Book of Jonah
The Pursuit is On
The Hazards of a Pursuit
A Whale of a Time
This Fish Represents Bondage and Bondage has Depth
The Roots of the Mountains
Three Types of Mountains
Mountain of Righteousness to Arise Above the Mountains of Carnality
The Rejection of Bondage
Blood Boiling Mad
We Must Guard Ourselves Against the Gourds of Life

Chapter 33: Repentance In the Book of Micah
The First to be Punished
Make Thee Bald
Balderdash

    The Balderdash of Repentance
    Chapter 34: Repentance In The Book of Nahum
    An Antecedent to Destruction

Chapter 35: Repentance in the Book of Habakkuk
    A Tale of Two Cities
    America's Ground Zero
    That Which Begs the Question
    America's Wake Up Call
    Judgment and Righteousness, Ignored
    Saviors of God
    The Exalted State of Carnality

Chapter 36: Repentance In the Book of Zephaniah
    A Time For repentance
    The Cycle of Grace

Chapter 37: Repentance In the Book of Haggai
    The Lollygagging Church
    The Dawdling Church
    Carnal Bruising
    Not Yet!
    Consider Your Ways
    Broken Spokes

Chapter 38: Repentance In the Book of Zechariah
    From a Tradition to a Transition
    Ishmael verses Isaac
    Desert Storm

Chapter 39: Repentance In the Book of Malachi
    The Burden of the Word is Repentance
    Pangs of Death
    From a Reproof to a Reproach
    The Skill of Debate
    Objection #1: In What Way Have You Loved Us?

Objection #2: How and in What Way Have We Despised Your Name?
Objection # 3: Since There is no Profit in It, Why Bother?
Objection #4: A Polluted Altar
Objection #5: What a Drudgery and Weariness This is!
Objection #6: Why Does He reject Our Offerings?
Objection #7: In What Way Have We Wearied Him?
Objection #8: How Shall We Return?
Objection #9: In What Way Have We Robbed you?
Answer a Question With a Question

Chapter 40: The Seven Furnaces of Mystery Babylon
Case Law: To Establish a Precedent as a Basis for an Argument
Furnace #1: Fear to be Replaced by Faith [trust]
Careful! Don't Get Incinerated
Furnace #2: The Furnace of Repentance & Sanctification
Getting Bloody in the Spirit
Blazing Your Own Trail
Furnace #3: Furnace of Forensic Cross-Examination
The Trial of One's Heart
Furnace #4: Increase Your Property Value
Furnace #5: The Righteous Judgment of the Church
Overcoming One's Hardness of Carnality
Gold of Faith and the Silver of Carnality
Furnace #6: The Furnace of Righteous Litigation
Flies Are Drawn to Uncovered Food
We Must Be Taught the Proper, Safe Use of Fire
A Rolled Newspaper
Furnace #7: The Wrath of God's Righteous Judgment
Carnality to Burn
Yellow is to Brass as Gold is to Faith
Closing Comments

Addendum: Truths of Repentance Itemized

Author's Preface

If you are anything like me, then you will appreciate provocative, spiritual insights which challenge established theological dogmas. For so many years, I have often mused over the many theological concepts of Bible doctrine. And through these years, I have asked spiritual leadership, church members and the "man on the street" to provide for me an acceptable explanation for such doctrines as faith, repentance, grace, righteousness, sanctification, consecration, etc. only to be given a vague, shallow answer from each individual and for each subject. In other words, they failed to provide me something fresh and new. Their answers parroted that which I already knew or have previously heard. To a great extent, I learned, through this census, that the truth of the gospel has been hidden under a false, philosophical pretense. Consequently, these answers only confirmed my heart felt witness of this reality.

The responses I received convinced me of three basic societal mind sets, which seemingly reflected a social conscience of illiteracy in varying degrees of biblical truth. To wit, it's common knowledge that the national illiteracy rate verges on thirty percent, and there are some counties within certain states where the illiteracy rate is even higher! For instance, it's been said that the illiteracy rate in Okmulgee County in Oklahoma is thirty-eight percent! If this is the case, then it is reasonable to suspect that such illiteracy would also bleed over and into the comprehension of scriptural truth. And given the worldly condition of the church en-masse today, I can understand why this is so.

As to faith, the answers provided by church leadership were the basic responses such as, "So then faith comes by hearing and hearing the word of God."(Rom.10:17) or "Now faith is the substance of things hoped for and is the evidence of things not seen." (Heb. 11:1) As to repentance, the best I have heard was simply turning around or turning your back on sin. Secondly, the church goer would refer to these basic Scriptures, but without a proper recitation of them, or they were uncertain of the scripture references themselves! Thirdly, the "man on the street," had his own vague, philosophical assumption as did a good majority of church folk! After all, as any church is a cross section of the community in which it is located, the parishioners are the very same people who come from that society.

I ask the reader to remember that this work is a personal revelation to me and that I do not claim to possess the final, definitive word on the theological subjects contained herein. Having stated this however, I do maintain that due to this extensive investigation of and about the many aspects and truths of a lifestyle of repentance, I do know far more about repentance than I have ever known or ever considered before.

This investigation, in the light of Scripture, contains the revelation of a Lifestyle of Repentance which embraces consecration, holiness, sanctification, righteousness, and godliness. You will find that this investigation is not an easy read, but it is hard hitting, strong and very provocative, and as you read through, your mind will be forced to consider new perspectives and concepts.

As you will learn, repentance presupposes carnality just as iniquity presupposes carnality. By presuppose, I mean too say that since iniquity is indigenous within the soul of each and every man, Almighty God's remedy for this carnal tragedy, is His gift of repentance to fallen humanity. He has granted repentance to mankind so that impenitent men would acknowledge their iniquity aka lie-based-thinking thereby, exposing and identifying this contamination, as an element of sin, within their souls. As pertaining to carnality, suffice it too say that this investigation contains carnal knowledge, a Roman Catholic expression, which simply refers to the knowledge of carnality. Moreover, repentance presupposes carnality just as revival presupposes a backsliding church. This then makes repentance a command of scripture for it is also the doctrine of God and as such, it is the knowledge of salvation. And I might add, that this knowledge of salvation will lead you to understand the duplicity of judgment as being for the salvation of the soul but against the iniquitous thoughts and the carnality within the soul.

Within these pages, you will find specific Truths of Repentance which are sequentially numbered. Each truth pertains to the matter of content and are revelations of and about repentance and the related attributes of it, such as godliness, righteousness, etc. As you absorb these Truths of Repentance you will experience personal transitions from the generally accepted doctrinal or theological traditions. In doing so, the scriptural knowledge that you once dismissed, shall become the scriptural knowledge you would now embrace! It is further noted, that as you digest this investigation, you will salt your soul with the word of God's righteousness as you assault your carnality. Consequently, your soul will be silently and secretly "cured" as you marinade your heart with God's anointed Word, which is His instructions in righteousness!

Let me conclude this by saying that the style of content and the flow of continuity which this investigation possesses, was written with a law enforcement officer's philosophical view point of jurisprudence, but from the standpoint of a prisoner. Therefore, it may be understood that the revelations of and about a lifestyle of repentance are substantiated with numerous truths that are true to Scripture, true to reason and true to life so that repentance would become to you, one over whelming and harmonious revelation.

Whereas, any prisoner becomes acquainted with the regimen of the correctional facility of which he is a resident, likewise you, the reader, shall also acquaint yourself with God's Incarceration Instructions for repentance is a lifestyle to live as a prisoner of Jesus Christ. Again, the investigative mind set, which any law enforcement officer possesses, shall be evident to you and having said this, you shall also recognize that the central theme of repentance has been written from the perspective of a prisoner.

This investigation contains many associations and metaphors common to life's encounters. Such similies will help clarify the truths which logic mandates must be demonstrated. As you progress through this work, you will find that your existing, entrenched philosophical opinions and other theological postulations will be challenged and hopefully brought to a logical consequence or outcome. Your emotions will be stirred, and it's my prayer for you that your conduct and your behavior will be changed as your carnality is suppressed.

I therefore, commend this work to you the reader, and to the corporate Body of Christ. It is my intent that you experience a sudden impact of such proportions that you will literally buckle at the knees! It is my intent also that your soul would be penetrated by the large caliber projectiles of divine revelation, so much so, that your soul would be perforated with the light of God's truth! I congratulate you dear reader, for having the courage to embark on a journey of the renewal of your mind and for a changed character.

As my brief census revealed, there are three classes of societal mind sets. Therefore, it is reasonable to assume that there are also three levels or conditions of mental acuity as the following will attest.

1. Idle minds are preoccupied with self, the material thing and others.

2. Average minds are preoccupied with situations, circumstances and events.

3. Great minds are preoccupied with concepts, ideas, and a

pursuit of knowledge and other disciplines of thought.

"The mind once expanded can never return to its original dimensions." Oliver Wendell Holmes

On a more personal note, I am an ordained minister who is also a retired California Highway Patrol Officer. I served the Golden State twelve years during which time Almighty God allowed me the distinct pleasure of ministry to the public. My style of writing, which is an economy of words, has come about due to the required disciplines of report writing, which law enforcement demands.

Introduction
The Birth of a Concept

It was Monday evening, January 11th, 1999. I attended a church service at Calvary Cathedral International in Fort Worth, Texas where Evangelist Stephen Hill was ministering. As he spoke, I was drawn to his eyes. They were as the eyes of a predator— as a lion on the prowl—who was about to pounce upon his unsuspecting prey! Although his message was titled, "I Have Sinned," the Holy Ghost spoke to my heart about repentance. Of course, to acknowledge that I had sinned leads me towards repentance, evangelistically speaking, but the Holy Ghost asked me, "Does merely admitting that I had sinned constitute true godly repentance?" I replied, "Since You asked me Lord, I guess not." The Spirit of God then said, "There are three things that will move the hand of Almighty God in the affairs of men. They are Faith, Rebellion and Repentance!" Then on Sunday, January 24, 1999 while again attending church service at Calvary Cathedral, International, I was introduced to a newly released book entitled, Judgment Day-2000 published by Treasure House. I purchased a copy and read it through twice in four days. Although its contents pertained to the world's intelligence and technical support systems pertaining to the "Y2K" dilemma back then, the Holy Ghost revealed to me a central theme which Almighty God wanted to address to the Body of Christ. That theme was repentance, the doctrine of God!

The Spirit of God used this book to confirm the commission which Almighty God had given me back on January 11th. The charge was to investigate these "three things" and document the revelations provided. So I did embark on a basic word study, taking each word separately. The first result was a book which I self published in the year 2000 entitled, The Aspects of the Audacity of Faith. subtitled Faith Ditties. Having completed this publication, I then commenced another word study (investigation) on rebellion. I soon discovered that our English word, *rebellion* is primarily of Old Testament origin and usage and that its New Testament equivalent is the English word, *disobedience*. This was determined through the Strong's Exhaustive Concordance. However, as I progressed through this particular investigation of rebellion, I realized that the carnality which resides in the soul of every man lurks about, lying in wait, waiting for opportunities to present itself in our conduct and our behavior (character). This awareness directed my attention to focus on repentance; the result being this investigative work which you are now reading.

This investigation is very comprehensive. It is the culmination of five years of intense thought and study in the classroom of the Holy Spirit. Other than a few ministers whom I respect and have used as sounding boards, no other individuals were involved in the writing of this work. Through the years, I actually became a bit of a recluse, for the Holy Ghost had steeled me away for this purpose. This work has proven itself worthy of ministry, in that I have consistently taught repentance during these past five years to the public, whether person to person or to an assembly and all with profound results!

No doubt that as time passes on, further revelations and spiritual truths will be acquired by His sagacious saints as Almighty God unfolds the breadth, length, depth, and heights of His concealed truths to them. It is therefore, my desire that as the grace and the knowledge of the things of God increase and continues to expand, that such knowledge will compel the Body of Christ to change her character, her views of traditional theology and language so as too reflect the pure image of The

Gospel, Jesus Christ, Himself.

For the purposes of clarity, I relied heavily on the Amplified Bible as a companion translation to the Authorized King James Version and the Scriptures used from the Amplified Version shall be self evident. All other Scriptures not so indicated were taken from the Authorized King James Version. Other research sources are indicated within and throughout the text of this investigation.

FREEDOM - The Liberty that Repentance Brings

Chapter 1
Theological Concepts and Ideas

I mentioned that the Holy Spirit spoke to me at a church service which I attended on Monday evening, January 11th 1999, in Fort Worth, Texas. I also stated that Almighty God had commissioned me to prepare this work that night. So in obedience, I did embark on this wonderful journey, cover to cover, through God's Word of faith, and in doing so, I positioned myself to receive these concepts and ideas which this investigation contains. These insights shall provide, to the prisoner of Jesus Christ, God's incarceration instructions, which is the Word of His righteousness. I trust that these instructions shall enable each saint to labor into God's rest, in that special place and position in Him, as a cell of penitence, that has remained seemingly inaccessible to the struggling saint. As was spoken to my heart, the Holy Spirit stated to me: "There are three things that shall move the hand of Almighty God in the affairs of men. They are faith, rebellion and repentance!" Since receiving this commission, I have learned that each of these spiritual attributes possess aspects, benefits and conditions. For example of faith, God's Word says:

Hebrews 11:6
"But without faith it is impossible to please Him: for he that cometh to God must believe that He is, and that He is a rewarder of them that diligently seek Him."

Hebrews 11:1
"Now faith is the substance of things hoped for and is the evidence of things not seen."

Romans 10:17
"So then faith cometh by hearing and hearing by the word of God."

As a benefit of faith, allow the following "faith ditty" which I took from my book, The Aspects of the Audacity of Faith, inspire your heart.

Faith therefore, is the currency of heaven, that median of exchange, that enables you and I to purchase God's grace, His [provision] for our triumphant living and our victorious life in Christ! In other words, faith, is heaven's currency! You see, the proportion of faith that is withdrawn is matched with the same proportion of faith deposited! In this way, our heavenly faith account is never depleted, but is fully available for our next faith withdrawal!

Of rebellion, God's Word says:

Isaiah 1:20
"But if ye refuse and rebel, ye shall be devoured with the sword: for the mouth of the Lord hath spoken it."

Isaiah 26:21
"For, behold, the Lord cometh out of his place to punish the inhabitants of the earth for their iniquity [rebellion, carnality]: the earth also shall disclose her blood, and shall no more cover her slain." (Brackets mine)

Romans 8:6 AMP
"Now the mind of the flesh [which is sense and reason without the Holy Spirit] is death [death that comprises all the miseries aris-

ing from sin, both here and hereafter]. But the mind of the Spirit the [Holy] Spirit is life and [soul] peace [both now and forever]."

It could be said then, that rebellion has a death benefit and this is a bonafide guarantee!

Psalm 18:20-26:
"The Lord rewarded me according to my righteousness; according to the cleanness of my hands hath he recompensed me. For I have kept the ways of the Lord, and have not wickedly departed from my God. For all his judgments were before me, and I did not put away his statutes from me. I was also upright before him, **and I kept myself from mine iniquity.** *Therefore hath the Lord recompensed me according to my righteousness, according to the cleanness of my hands in his eyesight. With the merciful thou wilt shew thyself merciful: with an upright man thou wilt shew thyself upright; With the pure thou wilt shew thyself pure:* **and with the froward thou wilt shew thyself froward."**
(emphasis mine)

Notice the word, *froward*. The Hebrew translation is *skolios*. It means "to be crooked." From this we get the term "scoliosis of the spine" which is a physical malady commonly seen as a curvature of the spine.

Of repentance, God's Word says:

2 Corinthians 7:10a
"For godly sorrow worketh repentance unto salvation not to be repented of:..."

Philippians 2:12b
"...work out your own salvation with fear and trembling."

Acts 20:21 AMP
"But constantly and earnestly I bore testimony both to Jews and Greeks, urging them to turn in repentance [that is due] to God and to have faith in our Lord Jesus Christ [that is due Him]."

Of the many Scriptures which this investigation contains regarding repentance, I have too say that these three repentance scriptures have served as a foundation upon which to build. *(cf. Eph. 2:20; 1 Tim. 6:19)*

Man's Traditional Precepts

Historically, mankind has based his living on precepts, which have become the foundation and tradition of generations before him. Such traditions have, over time, affixed themselves to religions and cultures that vary from people to people and nation to nation. As a result, value systems have risen by or through which each person and every society derives a sense of self worth and purpose. Such conditions of humanity are described as being demographic and psycho graphic. These terms refer to the societal constitution and social conscience in which people who think alike, speak alike and look alike naturally live alike. Genesis chapter 11 for example, provides the very first example of demographics and psycho graphics through the dispersion of that society. These people of antiquity, were forced to disperse by Almighty God for their disobedience to His command to dominate and subdue the earth.

The diversities of these value systems vacillate from one culture to another. Because of these varied systems, each society has identified for itself absolutes, be they despotic or democratic. And as such, these absolutes have defined the social morality which is unique to the character of each society or culture. Oftentimes however, people who are accustomed to their particular value system, misconstrue the precepts of that system to be truths when in reality, they are or may be just facts or legends. You see, facts apply themselves to life's scenarios, situations, and circumstances, while legends tend to be more imaginary pertaining to the things of folklore. It's for this reason that only facts are pertinent in a court of law. Emotional outbursts, opinions and individual philosophies are not relevant, judiciously. These facts and legends, in the guise of past traditions, whether distant or not, have become societal building blocks as well as the source of entrenched mind sets. Such mind sets are often illusions and illogical reasoning, which have become the seed beds for domestic and civil unrest.

There have been advances in civilizations as well. Inventions have dramatically altered and forever have changed or replaced the former things with the latter. This also applies to the New Testament Church. Foundational doctrines, denominational distinctions and interpretations of biblical text have often impaired the unity of the corporate Body of Christ and these have been the church's escort throughout the centuries. It is apparent then, that people have held to their old ways of thought and character, unique to the precept or their mind set, and have disregarded Biblical truth. And in so doing, they have set aside the possibility of increased knowledge and have surrendered their mind to universal skepticism or suspicion!

Pontius Pilate once asked Jesus, "What is truth?" Jesus said of Himself, *"I am the Way, the Truth and the Life."* (cf. John 14:6) The Bible further implies that the elect of God would be, *"sanctified by truth."* (cf. John 17:17) Notice that the Bible states "truth" and not facts! One day while in court, I overheard a question from one attorney to another. The question was, "Why are we required to raise our right hand when taking the oath to tell the truth, the whole truth and nothing but the truth, so help us God?" Neither attorney could answer this question. So I volunteered this response to their question. I said, "The reason that a witness is required to raise their right hand when swearing in is that Jesus Christ, Who is the Truth, sits at the right hand of the Father." *(cf. John 1:14; Heb. 10:12)* These two lawyers just sat there looking at me with their eyes fixed, as if they had just been zapped with a stun gun! Truths then, are spiritual absolutes and are eternal, whereas facts are worldly, ever changing and therefore, temporal.

As to the traditional church, there are those congregations who stubbornly hold to the liturgy, that which is considered to be sacred, ceremonial and ritualistic, by them. Yet there are other congregations who have embraced the liberal belief found in the charismatic movement. And still, even within the charismatic movement, there exists the elements of carnality and religious bondage which are not unique to these alone. It is therefore reasonable to deduce that as long as humanity is involved, such elements of the flesh [carnality] shall be found. Generally, and because of man's carnality, the dignity of the pulpit and its ministry, like water that has sought the path of least resistance, has trickled into a rendering of a "cornflake" gospel. Such renderings have diminished the impact and the strength of the true gospel message! In my opinion, the obvious state of the blinded denominational church confirms this observation.

Because I have been commissioned by providence to embark on this investigation, I begin with leadership whether secular of ecclesiastic. It is here, whether there be fault or not, that the judgment of Almighty God shall commence! Please note that a judgment, like an emotion, is neither good nor bad, positive nor negative, right nor wrong. It simply is! Judgment, or to judge, is a judicial expression and as such, must be applied in that context. Otherwise, an abuse of judgment will exist. For most of us, what we call a judgment is only an observation, but God's judgment is always just and right, where ours is biased and imperfect. In this investigation, you will learn of the duplicity of judgment which is both for and against. Where the first is so stated, the other is automatically implied.

Whenever a crime occurs, evidence is always left at the scene. The evidence is eventually collected and forensically investigated prior to the eventual trial. So in all actuality, there are two levels of investigation. The first occurs in the lab prior to the trial, while the second is a courtroom qualification. When you think of a witness testifying in court, he is sworn in as he takes the stand. The oath taken is an "implied consent," because the witness grants the court permission to cross examine him. Under thorough examination by the trial attorneys, the testimony given would be examined and qualified before it can be admitted as evidence. Through this examination process, which often takes hours, even days, the witness is grilled, because the human response taken is often a defensive posture. Or if the testimony lacks substance, then the testimony given must be shattered before the facts of the case are revealed. But more of this shall be covered later.

Things about and of the past, although esteemed by many, still possess a societal influence on the form, function and facility of any church or society. Such history must never be forgotten, but often such antiquated traditions must be revitalized with a fresh wind which the Holy Spirit is wanting to blow, especially upon the Church in these last days! This stale religion which I speak of, must be replaced with a fresh breeze of God! The people of God must set their hearts and souls to seek the Lord their God! They must arise from their passivity and build the sanctuary of the Lord upon the foundations of the apostles and the prophets! *(cf. Eph. 2:20; 1 Tim. 6:19)* I therefore, present to the Body of Christ, this investigation.

The revelations contained herein, are fresh, hot off the Holy Ghost press! My intent here is to present them to the Body of Christ as they were revealed to me. There are 257 "Truths of

Repentance." These truths shall transform your life! However, realistically, not all can be assimilated by the individual.

A Limited Grace Period is not an Age of Grace!

As a retired California Highway Patrol Officer, I can say that whenever a new traffic control device, law or city ordinance was introduced to the community, the citizens of that community needed time to acquaint themselves to the new intrusive device or law. They were granted a "limited grace period" for this purpose. Consider this: Whenever a "new thing" is either introduced, invented, learned or established, people generally experience a time of adjustment and transition. Such transitions often cause friction and outrage, because for most, change is difficult. Therefore, a limited grace period is often granted so that people may accommodate themselves to the "new thing."

Nobody likes change and therefore resistance is to be expected. This was especially the case with the Hebrew nation just delivered from four hundred years of Egyptian bondage! It was for this very reason that Moses had such a difficult time with this motley group and as a result of their continued disobedience, Moses spent the last forty years of his life writing the Pentateuch, the Talmud and the first five books of the Bible, as newly enacted laws which were designed to regulate societal order. These laws of God addressed moral depravity, selfishness, and carnality as the sin of the people, and research has revealed that Moses's intent was to reacquaint the Hebrew nation to the covenant keeping, Judge of the universe, the Lord their God!

As mentioned, the Pentateuch consists of five Books. They are Genesis, Exodus, Leviticus, Numbers and Deuteronomy. They are known as the "Mosaic law, the laws of Moses" or "the law" as referred to many times throughout Scripture. God knows what His Church has need of. As pertaining to the Hebrew nation just delivered, God was fully aware that time was required for

His chosen people to learn these laws and then to apply them to their livelihood. As it was for them, so it is for us today. We all require time to incorporate God's Word of truth into our lives, our hearts and our souls so that His will, His Word, and His ways would become evident in our lives. In this sense, it could be said that humanity is on probation! My question to you, dear saint, is this. How much time do you need and what does your heart felt conscience tell you about your relationship with Almighty God?

I use the term probation intentionally, for it basically infers an extended state of trial so long as a man lives. When I was a rookie law enforcement officer, I was required to serve two years probation. The intent being, to prove my worth to the uniform and profession and to also expose discrepancies within my character that could render me unsuitable and therefore possibly make me a discredit to the profession. Similarly, with regards to the fall of Adam and ever since then, humanity has been on probation with, I believe, the same import.

One way or the other, each of us shall be held accountable in this life! What we do here and now directly determines our destination then. *(cf. Gal. 6:8)* The grace period God gives us all is not an age [dispensation] of grace in the traditional, historical sense, but it is a probationary period for the individual, while he lives. And just as the authorities would know the length or duration of a grace period extended to the citizenry, likewise, Almighty God knows the exact date such a trial period shall conclude for the individual while he lives! This does not necessarily refer to the termination of one's life either, because Scripture does tell us that many have been given over to a reprobate mind, because they preferred not to retain the knowledge of God in their mind. *(cf. Rom. 1:28)* This grace period then, is the allotted time God has allowed each person to comply with His law of faith found in His Word of righteousness. This grace period does not require a life time to practice. However, to incorporate the Word of God does! In this, ignorance of the law is never an excuse! In other words, our continued obedience to the terms and conditions of the Word of God is the prerequisite of our redemption, our final salvation. The kingdom of God is based upon the moral government of God and continued obedience to its laws is a condition and a qualification to the favor of God. This intimates that God's commands are paralleled to His promises! And as for The Church, all the promises of God hinge upon faith and repentance, for they go hand in hand. Therefore, judgment and righteousness, as well as credibility and integrity go hand in hand, much like a covenant between two people go hand in hand.

The Age of Grace or The Age of Promiscuity

It appears that the denominational church has erred in its general theology regarding the dispensation of grace. Generally, this miscue infers that this age, as pertaining to grace, is a dispensation of time, specifically throughout the church age. However, scripture denotes a dispensation of grace to be more of a spiritual commodity or ingredient of God, for ministry during the life of a saint and not necessarily an epoch of time. *(cf. Eph. 3:2-4)* Shallow understanding and comprehension of the aspects of grace are therefore evident. *God's grace to His Church is a constitutional necessity, that is based upon a covenant relationship* for without it, His Church would not be equipped.

We tend to emphasize grace, but overlook faith and repentance! The traditional church must understand that God's grace is eternal, even as He is. His grace co-exists with Him. Grace originates from Him, therefore, God and His grace are one! God's grace to man is embodied in the person of His Son, Jesus Christ Who is the Word of His grace made flesh! *(cf. John 1:14)*

A Topical Investigation of Grace

Grace is first seen through the eye of faith. It is the evidence or the manifestation of faith, just as our thoughts are things and our words are containers. Grace is more than unmerited favor, which is how it is predominantly defined. It is multifaceted, even as God! Too say that grace is simply God's unmerited favor, is too say, "Look there's an iceberg!" We forget that three-fourths of it is still unseen beneath the surface. Just as the top one-quarter of the iceberg is seen above the water, mariners must always remember to give it a wide girth. So it is with grace. Grace is so much more than unmerited favor! The grace of God is His divine influence upon the heart and it's reflection in life. (Vine's Expository Dictionary, page 170) Although it is correct to say that God's grace is His unmerited favor, it is not entirely accurate. It is for this reason that the Body of Christ must understand and comprehend God's grace! In this way, grace becomes tangible although it is spiritual. You see, *grace is God's divine gratuity to humanity!* When I was a uniformed officer, the Government Code of California prohibited me or any uniformed officer from receiving gratuities from the general public, as said gifts could possibly incur a conflict of interest between the agency and the public it serves. However with God, there is no conflict of interest, when His grace is accepted and received! But a conflict of interest shall exist whenever God's grace is denied, frustrated or rejected, and I apply this towards a lifestyle of repentance, specifically!

Galatians 2:21
"[Therefore, I do not treat God's gracious gift as something of minor importance and defeat its purpose]; I do not set aside and invalidate and frustrate and nullify the grace (unmerited favor) of God..."

The Nomenclature of Grace

When I was in the Marine Corps, I became acquainted with the word, nomenclature. It basically pertains to the description of a thing which included its dimensions, its caliber, its weight, etc. For instance, the nomenclature of an M-14 assault rifle is: a magazine fed, gas operated, air cooled, shoulder weapon whose projectile is a 7.62 caliber, etc. Generally, I learned of the breakdown and the nomenclature of my rifle while in class, however I became proficient with my shoulder weapon while out on the "grinder" or while out at the firing range. And so it is with all things spiritual. We learn of them in the classroom of the Holy Spirit, but we become proficient with them out in the grinder called life! Since God's grace is a spiritual thing of His, then it to must be broken down and described, for it too has a nomenclature. Therefore, grace is defined and described to be "kindness, favor, pleasant, precious, well-favored, to bend or stoop down to in kindness to an inferior, to bestow, to implore, to move to favor by petition, beseech, deal, to give, in treat, be merciful, have pity upon, make supplication." (Strong's Exhaustive Concordance Hebrew, ref. #2580; page 430)

God's grace is also defined as and described to be, "divine gratuity, free gift, spiritual endowment, religious qualification, deliverance from danger or passion, joy, pleasure, benefit, gift, divine influence upon the heart and its reflections in life." (Strong's Exhaustive Concordance Greek ref. #5485, 5486; page 430)

Grace Applications

The following commentaries concerning "Objective" and "Subjective" grace was extracted in part from the Vine's Expository Dictionary, page 170 and the related passages of Scripture. There are two basic classes of grace. They are Objective Grace and Subjective Grace. Where the former is general, the later is more specific. And each is further broken down according to the method of use or application.

Objective grace is that aspect of grace which is dispensed to bestow or occasion pleasure, delight or causes favored regard. Grace is further broken down as applied to:
- 1) beauty or the graciousness of a person or an act of kindness.
- 2) grace for ministry
- 3) a state of grace as it applies to knowledge and understanding.
- 4) deeds of grace as applied to donations, administrations and contributions.
- 5) elections of grace as applied to predestination.

Subjective grace applies to that which is bestowed. It is the friendly disposition from which kindly acts proceed. Where objective grace is generally observed or received by others, subjective grace pertains to the individual as the giver. Subjective grace may also be applicable to all the aspects of objective grace. Furthermore, grace is also referred to as promises, riches and inheritance. *(Rom. 4:13, 20-21, 9:23; Eph. 1:18, 1:11, 18, 3:8; Deut. 4:20; Col. 1:12, respectively)*

The following Scriptures apply to Objective Grace as indicated.
- 1. Beauty or Graciousness of a Person or an Act:

Genesis 43:29b
"...And he said, God be gracious unto thee, my son."

Exodus 33:19
"And he said, I will make all my goodness to pass before thee, and I will proclaim the name of the Lord before thee; and will be gracious to whom I will be gracious, and will shew mercy on whom I will shew mercy."

Proverbs 1:9
"For they shall be an ornament of grace unto thy head and chains about thy neck"

Proverbs 4:9
"She [Wisdom] shall give to thine head an ornament of grace: a crown of glory shall she deliver to thee."

- 2. Grace for Ministry:

Ephesians 3:1-4
*"For this cause I Paul, the prisoner of Jesus Christ for you gentiles, If ye have heard of the dispensation of the grace of God **which is given me** to you-ward: how that by revelation he made known unto me the mystery; ...ye may understand my knowledge in the mystery of Christ."* (emphasis mine)

Ephesians 3:7
"Whereof I was made a minister, according to the gift of the grace of God given unto me by the effectual working of his power."

Ephesians 2:7-9
"That in the ages to come he might shew the exceeding riches of his grace in his kindness towards us, through Christ Jesus. For by grace are ye saved, through faith and not of yourselves: it is the gift of God: not of works lest any man should boast."

1 Timothy 1:12
"And I thank Christ Jesus our Lord, who hath enabled me, for that he counted me faithful, putting me in the ministry;"

Romans 1:5-7
"By whom we have received grace and apostleship, for obedi-

ence to the faith among all nations, for his name: Among whom are ye also the called of Jesus Christ: To all that be in Rome, beloved of God, called to be saints: Grace to you and peace from God our Father, and the Lord Jesus Christ."

1 Corinthians 3:10a
"According to the grace of God given unto me, as a wise master builder..."(cf. Rom. 12:6, 15:15-16; Gal. 2:9)

- 3. State of Grace as Applied to Knowledge and Understanding:

Hosea 4:6 AMP
"My people are destroyed for lack of knowledge; because you [the priestly nation] have rejected knowledge, I will also reject you that you shall be no priest to Me; seeing you have forgotten the law of your God, I will also forget your children."

2 Peter 3:18a
"But grow in grace and the knowledge of our Lord and Saviour Jesus Christ..."

Ephesians 1:17-18
"That the God of our Lord Jesus Christ, the Father of glory, may give unto you the Spirit of wisdom and revelation in the knowledge of him: the eyes of your understanding being enlightened; that ye may know what is the hope of his calling, and what the riches of the glory of his inheritance in the saints,"

- 4. Deeds of Grace:

1 Corinthians 16:3 AMP
"And when I arrive, I will send on those whom you approve and

authorize with credentials to carry your gift [of charity] to Jerusalem."

2 Corinthians 8:6 AMP
"So much so that we have urged Titus that as he began it, he should also complete this beneficent and gracious contribution among you [the church at Corinth]."

2 Corinthians 9:6-9
"But this I say, He which soweth sparingly shall reap also sparingly; and he which soweth bountifully shall also reap bountifully. Every man according as he purposeth in his heart, so let him give; not grudgingly, or of necessity: for God loveth a cheerful giver. And God is able to make all grace abound toward you; that ye, always having all sufficiency in all things, may abound to every good work: (As it is written, He hath dispersed abroad; he hath given to the poor: his righteousness remaineth forever...)"

- 5. Elections of Grace as Applied to Predestination and Salvation:

Exodus 6:7
"And I will take you to me for a people, and I will be to you a God: and ye shall know that I am the Lord your God, which bringeth you out from under the burdens of the Egyptians."

Deuteronomy 7:6
"For thou art an holy people unto the Lord thy God: the Lord thy God hath chosen thee to be a special people unto himself, above all people that are upon the face of the earth."

Ephesians 1:4-7
"According as he hath chosen us in him before the foundation of the world, that we should be holy and without blame before him

in love: Having predestinated us unto the adoption of children by Jesus Christ to himself, according to his good pleasure of his will, to the praise of the glory of his grace, wherein he hath made us accepted in the beloved. In whom we have redemption through his blood, the forgive-ness of sins, according to the riches of his grace:" (cf. Deut. 4:37; Mat. 25:34; John 15:16; Gal. 4:30; 1 Pet. 1:2)

Contrasts to/of Grace

To recognize grace, whether objective or subjective, the opposite or its contrast must be considered. In doing so, grace becomes evident in your life, personally so that God's grace to you, becomes stabilized, validated and guaranteed! Moreover, audacious faith is the means, method and the manner by which you may have bold access or entry into God's grace! Grace therefore, stands in contrast to all that is worldly! *(Rom. 4:16, 5:2; 2 Cor. 8:9)* The following examples will make this evident.

- 1. Debt to the world vs. indebtedness to God. *(cf. Rom. 4:4, 8:12; Gal. 5:3)*
- 2. Love of the world vs. love of God and the things of God. *(cf. 1 John 2:15; James 1:27b; 4:4)* Works of the Flesh vs. Fruit of the Spirit. *(cf. Gal. 5:17-23)*
- 3. Works of Religion vs. Works of God. *(cf. Rom. 11:6; Gal. 2:16; James 2:14-26)*
- 4. Worldly Fame vs. Godly Acclaim. *(cf. James 2:1-6; Mal. 2:9; Micah 3:11-12; 1 Tim. 5:12)*
- 5. Inconsideration vs. Greetings and Salutations. See Paul's Epistles.
- 6. Carnal Mindedness vs. Grace (spiritual) Mindedness. *(cf. Hos. 4:6; Rom. 8:4-8; 1 Cor. 3:14-1, 4:1-4)*

Itemized Bipolarities of Grace

Type/anti-type, Christ/anti-Christ, positive/negative, right/wrong, black/white, light/dark, freedom/ imprisonment, liberty/bondage, thesis/antithesis, real/fake, love/hate, rich/poor, prosperity/poverty, grace/law, works/fruit.

As recorded in the Old Testament, grace is basically applied to sight, vision, or spiritual perception. However, there are four verses that distinguish grace to be other than visual acuity. They are:

- 1. Proverbs. 4:9, depicts grace as an ornament.
- 2. Jeremiah 31:2, depicts grace to be either a place of rest or exile.
- 3. Ezra 4:1-5, depicts grace to be an gift or ability to resist opposition.
- 4. Zechariah 4:7, depicts grace to be spirit.

As anyone would expect, a credible investigation should answer specific questions such as who, what, when, where, why, how. Having completed this topical investigation of grace, let us now answer these questions for ourselves.

Who is grace? God the Father and Jesus Christ His Son. *(cf. John 1:14)*

What is grace? At the very least, grace is identified as God's unmerited favor. But it is so much more!

When is grace? Grace is seasonal, and yet it remains eternal as God is eternal. Grace is given as a spiritual endowment for specific tasks and charges. It is also given for a specified period of time or for a specific purpose. *(cf. Zech. 12:10-14; Ezra 9:8)*

Where is grace? Grace originates from Almighty God and is dispensed to humanity through faith in Jesus Christ. Therefore, grace may be found in men as an ornament of God's character in their hearts and as the knowledge of God in their minds.

Why is grace? For God so loved the world... Primarily, grace exists because God loves us, however, it is also a constitutional necessity based upon a covenant relationship.

How is grace? Grace, both objective and subjective, is obtained through audacious faith of the saint and is given as a sovereign act and as a constitutional condition according to the terms of God's will, generally and specifically.

You see, for the saint, God's grace is the evidence of his faith! Speaking from my own experience, I give you this "faith (grace) ditty" from my book, "The Aspects of the Audacity of Faith." *When I was a sinner, I was saved by God's grace, as there was no other way it could be; but now that I am a saint, I am saved by my faith!*

1 Peter 1:9-10
"Receiving the end of your faith, even the salvation of your souls. Of which salvation the prophets have enquired and searched diligently, who prophesied of the grace [of redemption] that should come unto you:" (cf. John 3:15, 5:24, 11:25, 12:46, 20:31; Rom. 4:16, 10:9; 2 Tim. 3:15; James 1:21) (brackets mine)

This "age of grace" has been portrayed as a dispensation of time wherein God shows His forgiveness, mercy and compassion towards all of "Carnal Christianity" which is another bit of church jargon. This age is not an age of rest! Yet pulpit theology has seemingly adopted a presumptuous attitude, that Jesus Christ has done it all for us and there is nothing left for His church to do! Holding to this current presumption, why then did the Apostle Paul tell us to put on the "armor of God" in Ephesians 6? Why did he inform us that the "weapons of our warfare are not carnal" in 2 Corinthians 10? Why then did he tell young Timothy to "Fight the good fight of faith" in 1 Timothy 6? Why then did Paul tell Timothy "To be a good soldier enduring hardships and suffering" as found in 2 Timothy 2? Finally, why then did the Apostle Peter tell the Church to, "Grow in grace" in 2 Peter 3 or James tell the Church that "God gives more grace to the humble" in James 4:6? This presumption is dangerous and foolish!

Hebrews 4:1, 2
"The same gospel message preached today was also preached to them, but the word preached did not profit them not being mixed with faith."

Paul said this during the first decades of the early church, which did not have the written text of the New Testament scriptures! In other words, he was saying that the Old Testament text pointed to Jesus Christ and testified of Him.

It appears then, that the doctrinal belief of an "age of grace" has been a means to justify, excuse or make allowances for liberal, sloppy, carnal thinking and living in this church age! Although such promiscuous activity is often discouraged from the pulpits, this greasy grace nonetheless ought to be more appropriately called an *age of promiscuity*. You see, Almighty God, demands that His Church be clothed in faith and repentance as a chaste virgin, but the reality is that the worldly church, in a carnal sense, has become a harlot!

As any bride is female, she would be espoused to her bridegroom. Culturally, this bride would have the choice to be betrothed singularly and solely to her bridegroom. She could be unfaithful to him in his absence and he may never know of her infidelity. It is evident then, that too many, who occupy the pews of denominational churches, which comprise the New Testament Church, call themselves "Christians." They surmise that attending church services or possessing denominational membership qualifies them for salvation. They fail to realize that the word, "Christian" is a universal term that has been abused and misused. Its origin dates back when the Roman authority labeled the true followers of Christ with scorn. (Vine's Expository Dictionary 191). To wit, Jesus Christ never identified or called His followers "Christians!" Rather, He did call them disciples, laborers, saints, the elect and friends, etc. So to be a saint and a heir of the promises and inheritance of God requires us to be disciples of the faith of faithful Abraham, whose obedient faith was accounted to him as righteousness. *(cf. Rom. 4:9)* The true Bride of Christ are those saints of God who love Him and are of this faith, who stagger not from the one, true faith and who are fully persuaded. *(cf. Rom. 4:13-16)*

It must be noted that godly people are the Church and not a denomination, itself. When we choose to stagger through unbelief, in effect, we are disputing with God! Such a mind set tells God, "I am filing a law suit against you!" (Matthew Henry's Commentary, page 2203, col. 2) This statement implies that an appeal has been made to neutralize or annul the credibility of God's argument against impenitent man! For instance, the word, *stagger* means: "to sue at the law, call in question." (Strong's Exhaustive Concordance, Greek # 1252 cf. 2919, pages 22 and 43). I believe the reason for this mind set is simply, people don't want to be told what to do! They state, "I know my rights! This is a free nation! Just who are you to tell me what to do?" It seems that everybody has rights, but obligations and personal integrity are foreign concepts! The "rights" a carnally minded man may ascribe to in his selfishness, does not imply or infer that the selfish should have their way at the expense of others! These "rights" do imply however, that everyone has the right to expect decency and over all good conduct and behavior from one another.

I have heard inferences, primarily from the pulpit, that loosely support the distorted church view of the term "Carnal Christian." I do agree and therefore do believe that God is forgiving, full of mercy and compassion for each and every human being, but His goodness towards us is conditioned upon our continual obedience to the terms and conditions of His Word. Salvation then is conditioned by faith and repentance, not assumptions which originate from "piece meal theology." Conditions which are founded upon the specific knowledge of the Word of God and even more specifically, with regards to the knowledge of salvation.

Church Distinctions

For the purposes of this investigation, I wish to make a distinction between the New Testament Church and the traditional denominational churches. Where the New Testament Church is defined by faith and repentance, the more liberal, denominational churches are nothing more than churches of the New Testament existing within this church age, and are usually defined by their institutional doctrine and dogma. Aside from the seven letters written to the seven churches found in the book of Revelation, nowhere in Scripture shall any denomination or religious institution be found, although the Pauline epistles [letters] were written to churches in specific localities. Such inferences as "this denominational faith" or "that institutional doctrine" is confusing. Our telephone directories supports this fact! Scripture states that there is only one Lord, one faith and one baptism! *(cf. Eph. 4:5)* To identify a denomination, as a faith in addition to or estranged from true, godly faith, is putting a priority upon that denomination and its doctrine over the Word of God! For the purposes of this investigation then, I stipulate that what a doctrine is to a literal document, a dogma is to a denominational influence! *(cf. Mk. 7:7-13)*

Piece meal theology is a pretext, because the Word of God is taken out of context! What is left is confusion, competition and promiscuity and the Church remains ignorant of the wiles of deceit, due to this presumptuous state that is very evident within this "information age." Isn't it interesting that, in this computer age, people are given more to the "Information Highway" and the data therein, which is outdated within a year, and yet are predominantly ignorant of the "King's Highway" which shall never be outdated! Whereas, deceit is an abuse of truth, similarly promiscuity is an abuse of liberty!

Hosea 4:6
"My people are destroyed for lack of knowledge: because thou hast rejected knowledge, I will also reject thee, that thou shalt be no priest to me: seeing thou hast forgotten the law of thy God, I will also forget thy children."

James 1:21b AMP
"...and in a humble (gentle, modest) spirit receive and welcome the word which implanted and rooted [in your hearts] contain the power to save your souls."

Philemon 6 AMP
"[And I pray] that the participation in and sharing of your faith may produce and promote full recognition and appreciation and understanding and precise knowledge of every good [thing] that is ours in [our identification with] Christ Jesus and unto His glory."

An Implanted Heart is a Saved Soul

All things being equal, everyone has general knowledge, but not all have revelation knowledge! Moses, for example, was groomed in the court of Pharaoh. Although he was adopted, he was an equal with Pharaoh's son, named Rameses. Because Moses was his equal, he could not speak anything to Rameses other than that which was generally known by each. It wasn't until God commissioned Moses to return to Pharaoh with specific revelation knowledge! It is also true for us today. Specific knowledge, for this investigation, is revelation knowledge. Until such knowledge is obtained, with all things being equal, no one could say anything more than what is generally known. Specific knowledge, therefore, breaks the impasse of finite wisdom!

I read a quotation sometime ago which relates to this very well. The statement is: "Idle minds gossip, average minds talk of situations, events and circumstances, but great minds speak of ideas, concepts and theories." (author unknown) The writer and physician of the nineteenth century, Oliver Wendell Holmes once said, "The mind once expanded, can never return to its original dimensions." This investigation shall expand your mind! What "psychedelic" is to blowing your mind, Scripture will enlighten your mind. It will shatter the stalemate wherein nominal thinking and living exist! Furthermore, you shall soon notice a disgust with all that is generally known and accepted. As you continue to read and then apply the truths contained within this work, you shall enlarge and implant your heart and save your soul from its distress! *(cf. Psa. 4:1)*

For the most part, the denominational church structure has relied upon floppy faith to get greasy grace in this age of promiscuity. Pride, emotional outbursts, offenses and carnal mind sets have become the basis for all differences! These unregenerate mind sets have only strengthened the strongholds of man's carnality in the guise of his personal opinions and philosophies, within the institutionalized church. As long as men remain carnal, they shall remain promiscuous. The intent of this work is to break the back of carnality's grip and its predominant influence upon the church. As this is done, promiscuity, as a state of carnality, shall deteriorate and God's righteousness shall become a reality to humanity.

With regards to the "Carnal Christian" to be fair, I do acknowledge that converts can remain, become and are carnal, but so is everyone else. Fallen humanity possesses a carnality that lurks within the depths and faculties of the soul of every human being. The word, *carnivorous* for example, means "a flesh or meat eating animal." From this is derived the word, *carnal* which implies that people have within their souls a flesh nature which is unique to their fallen condition. The Bible speaks of it as iniquity and the works of the flesh. *(cf. Isa. 22:14; Gal. 5:17)*

Seemingly, the denominational church has made its own

distinction between saintly carnality and worldly carnality and yet the Bible makes no such distinction at all. For example, the word, *childish* means, "the immature conduct and behavior of an adult. Such observed or known conduct and behavior is considered to be abhorrent to other mature adults, because adults expect more maturity from one another." Childish as applied to a young child is expected by adults due to his youth. However, to see an adult act like a child in their misunderstanding or one who has not put away childish things is an insult to other mature adults." (Webster's)

1 Corinthians 13:11 AMP
"When I was a child, I talked like a child, I thought like a child, I reasoned like a child; now that I have become a man, I am done with childish ways and have set them aside."

1 Corinthian 14:20 AMP
"Brethren, do not be children [immature] in your thinking; continue to be babes in [matters of] evil, but in your minds be mature [men]."

God the Father expects His people to grow in grace and into spiritual maturity and yet there are those who have not! Our churches are filled with immature converts in that they are still babes who can only digest pre-chewed food, (milk) and this meaning is not intended towards the newly converted! The church has forgotten that God's grace and spiritual maturity facilitates their redemption!

Romans 8:5, 6 AMP
"For those who are according to the flesh and [controlled by its unholy desires], **set their minds** *on and pursue those things which gratify the flesh. But those who are according to the Spirit*

and *[controlled by the desires] of the Spirit,* **set their minds** *on and seek those things which gratify the (Holy) Spirit. Now the mind of the flesh [which is sense and reason without the Holy Spirit] is death; death that comprises all the miseries arising from sin,* **both here and hereafter.** *But the mind of the (Holy) Spirit is life and soul-peace [both now and forever]." (cf. Gal. 5:19-21)* (emphasis mine)

Considering this then, there does exist a connection between saintly carnality and worldly carnality. Both apply towards a lack of spiritual development in ones character. *What a character trait may be to an individual, carnality is to a character flaw and a flawed human nature!* As long as people remain on earth, they shall contend with their carnality as that residue of sin! Just because a person may be converted, does not obstruct his carnality. It is for this reason that the Word of God was written, to address carnality, which is the seed bed for sin, unto the saving of souls! If a person chooses to remain carnally minded, in spite of all of God's efforts to save him, then that person shall die in his carnality, because he has given his mind over to universal scepticism.

The following Scriptures substantiate the free will choice of carnal man, because he has given his mind over to such uncertainty and therefore possesses a mistrust of God. For purposes of clarity, I have injected these verses with brackets to support this truth. Either way, man's choice to do and act in compliance to the terms and the conditions of God's Word, or his choice to rebel in his carnality against them, remains his choice to do and act, alone. As they say, "The choice is yours!" I trust that you will notice that Satan has nothing to do with our carnal ways, save the fact that since the fall of Adam and Eve, carnality has been etched in the soul of every man.

James 1:21 AMP
"So [you, yourself choose, as an act of your will to] get rid of all [of your] uncleanness and the rampant outgrowth of [your] wickedness, and in a humble (gentile, modest) spirit [of your mind, you choose to] receive and welcome the Word which implanted and rooted [in your hearts] contains the power to save your souls."

1 Corinthians 15:50
"Now this I say, brethren, that flesh and blood [all that is carnal] cannot inherit the kingdom of God; neither doth corruption inherit incorruption." (cf. 1 Pet. 4:17-18)

Galatians 6:8
"For he that [hath chosen as an act and a decision of his will to] soweth to his flesh shall of the flesh reap corruption; but he that [hath chosen as an act and a decision of his will to] soweth to the Spirit shall of the Spirit reap everlasting life." (cf. Luke 16:25,26)

Heaven's Court

It is clear that according to Scripture, there does exist a throne in heaven and a courtroom in which all who have failed to please God, in and through faith and repentance, shall be sentenced in accordance to their carnal conduct and behavior! It is therefore reasonable to say that John, the beloved Apostle, saw all that the book of Revelations describes and portrays. Almighty God, upon enlightening his mind, enabled John to know and perceive this prophetic truth with the eye of his reason (mind) and through the eye of faith. That God presented His argument to John's intellect, as a basis for His judgment against the carnality of impenitent men, reveals that Almighty God speaks with intelligent men, as one intelligent being to another. And the evidence which He has compiled against humanity as a whole, has convinced John of this argument for the sentencing of those who choose to remain stubbornly impenitent.

Revelation 20:11-12
"And I saw a great white throne, and him that sat on it, from whose face the earth and heaven fled away; and there was found no place for them. And I saw the dead, small and great, stand before God; and the books were opened: and another book was opened, which is the book of life: and the dead were judged out of those things which were written in the books according to their works."

Revelation 3:5 AMP
"He that [has chosen as an act or decision of his will to] over cometh, the same shall be clothed in white raiment; and I will not [be obliged, compelled or forced as a response to his decision or choice of his will to act or do] blot out his name out of the book of life; but I will confess his name before my Father, and before the angels."

Revelation 21:27 AMP
"And there shall in no wise [case] enter into it anything [or anyone] that defileth, neither whatsoever [that has chosen as a decision or act of his will to] worketh abomination, or maketh a lie; but they [who have chosen, as an act or decision of their will] which are written in the Lamb's book of life."

Revelation 20:12 AMP
"...And the dead were judged (sentenced) by what they had [chosen to do as an act or decision of their will] [their whole way of feeling and acting, their aims and endeavors as a consequence of their choices which were the impulsive acts and decisions of their will] in accordance with what was recorded in the books."

Revelation 20:13b AMP
"...and all were tried and their cases determined by what they had done according to their motives, aims and works."

Exodus 32:33
"And the Lord said unto Moses, Whosoever hath [chosen as an act or decision of his will to] sinned against me, him will I blot out of my book [because he has obliged Me to do so]." (brackets mine)

Carnal Attitudes and Hostile Mind Sets

We all have either stated or heard, "Ignorance of the law is no excuse." As a former California Highway Patrol Officer, I have been amazed at the motoring public's arrogance and presumption towards the laws and the officer enforcing them. Truly, what we purposely refuse to know can hurt us! For example, I have had encounters with violators who stated, "I know what the vehicle code says!" or "Why don't you stop a real criminal or investigate a real crime!" or "Let me have your name and badge number! I'm going to report you to your supervisor!" or "I'm going to speak to my attorney!" or "You stopped me just because I'm black!" Now, I'm sure that you the reader have never made such foolish remarks to an officer or haven't you? Such carnal attitudes and hostile mind sets exist in the church! This is what God's Word means by stagger! *(cf. Rom. 4:20)* Abraham never staggered, but he was fully persuaded! You see, any church congregation is a cross section of its own community as a whole, and just as such carnality runs rampant in the streets of society, so does this hostility exist within the aisles of the church!

Often I have, under the color of authority, assisted spiritual leadership at their very carnal best! From pastors whom I had the pleasure arresting for auto theft, to others involved with smuggling. Occasionally, I've assisted some church leaders who were stranded on the freeway or on a roadside kicking up a storm, and yelling all kinds of expletives at there vehicle or to their passengers! What has been a real joy for me was to suddenly arrive at a scene and catch my own leadership at their very carnal best, only to see their countenance do a complete "180." Or the "brother or sister" whom I have stopped for an observed moving violation, only to be patronized or scolded by him or her as I wrote out the citation!

The Elements of Criminal and Civil Law
James 4:17
"Therefore, to him who knoweth to do good, and doeth it not, to him it is sin."

1 John 3:4
"Whosoever committeth sin transgresseth also the law: for sin is the transgression of the law."

1 John 5:17
"All unrighteousness is sin: and there is a sin not onto death."

There are basically two categories of crime. They are criminal and civil. In my estimation, and for the purpose of illustration and explanation, I want you too know that the crime of commission applies to the penal code, while the crime of omission applies to the civil code and both possess a moral obligation towards our fellow man. Penal crime for example, is defined as being either an infraction, a misdemeanor or a felony. And each of these is further defined according to the severity of the act. With each, there exists elements, the *corpus delicti*. This is a Latin phrase which means, the "elements (body) of a crime." These elements are recorded in, the penal and the statutory codes as substance, in accordance to perpetrated acts against individuals and society as a whole.

Any criminal or civil offense must possess particular substance, which supports and undergirds the elements of the specified crime or offense committed. The crime scene evidence collected, must meet the elements so established in law and once determined, the case is brought to trial. It is said that such a case is "bound over for trial" to determine its credibility for litigation. In their preparations for trial, attorneys would research Case Law and Statute Law so as to strengthen their clients claim. Therefore, as we have already seen through Scripture, a person must prepare his case ahead of time for the upcoming trial!

Through this investigation of repentance, you will discover that God's Word possesses both Case Law and Statute Law. Whereas, Case Law is the compilation of previously adjudicated trails in which a past precedence has been established through the final decisions of the court, likewise, the Bible is also a compilation of divine judgments against the criminal activity of impenitent humanity. Its been said, "If you want to know how or what Almighty God is going to do with humanity today, just look back at what and how He dealt with humanity then!" Furthermore, Statute law applies to the strict adherence to the enacted laws of the land, just as God expects His Church to obey His statutes and precepts! Therefore, what the righteousness of God is to His Word and to the spirit [of the law], the law of the land is to natural man, and his compliance "to the spirit" of the criminal and civil law so established.

Iniquity is to a Guilty Mind

"And it came to pass..." is a phrase frequently found in Scripture. This phrase addresses the life time of our living on this earth. Whether we choose to live uprightly before God or to squander our lives presumptuously in wickedness and in our carnality, is an individual issue. But in criminal law, there is a term known as "criminal intent." *Mens Rea* is its Latin equiva-

lent which means, "guilty mind." It is the state of mind accompanying the particular act defined as criminal. The exact degree of criminal intent can only be determined after an forensic investigation. But please understand that what people experience and know in common with the judicial system presently, parallels the Great High Court—the Great White Throne Judgment of Revelations! Just as evidence is presented in court, so too shall the evidence of the iniquities of a guilty mind and the transgressions of a wicked life, be presented before the Supreme Court of heaven! You see, humanity is being investigated! Why do you suppose that our gifts and callings are without repentance? These provisions of providence shall be introduced as evidence against us, because the substance of our neglect supports our aims, motives and endeavors! Therefore, the elements of criminal law mirror the reality of our iniquities and transgressions! Where there is a law, there is transgression and the transgression instigated, tends towards the wrath of God!

Romans 4:15 AMP
"For the Law results in [divine] wrath, but where there is no law there is no transgression [of it either]."

Romans 11:29
"For the gifts and callings of God are without repentance."

Psalm 90:8
"Thou hast set our iniquities before thee, our secret sins in the light of thy countenance." (cf. 2 Chron. 16:9; Amos 9:8-10; Rev. 20:11-15)

The Seventh Day

Hebrews 4:4
"For he spake in a certain place of the seventh day on this wise,

and God did rest the seventh day from all his works." (cf. Gen. 2:2)

God's Word teaches that there is a *certain* place and an *appointed* day. That place is the kingdom of God and that appointed day is the seventh millennium in which the saints of God shall obtain their eternal rest. This rest is a habitation and a position in God that is acquired through faith and repentance. *(cf. Psalm 91:1-2, 9)* Just as Monday precedes Tuesday, likewise, the sixth day precedes the seventh. Its akin to the "law of necessity" also known as "cause and effect." Whatever conduct and behavior people demonstrate on earth here and now, as a causation, shall determine the reward of their eternal destination then, in the hereafter!

The Scripture above denotes that God did rest on the seventh day. This also implies that the true saints of God shall also enter into His rest. *(cf. Heb. 4:7-10)* Since this is the case, then it is reasonable to say that the seventh day is future, contextually speaking. Therefore, it is also apparent that presently, the New Testament Church is still occupying a certain place [earth] and that His Church is at the threshold of that appointed day, the seventh millennium, which also implies that His Church is still living in the sixth day. Since Almighty God is eternal and He occupies eternity, then it is correct to say that all that God is and has also continues throughout infinity. Therefore, all of God's provisions are absolute truths and humanity should consider them as such. God's Word must never be set aside by our views for expediency, because His commands are His expressed judgments to us which reveal, with unerring certainty, the true path of expediency as that path of life. With God, there are no contingencies for He changes not. However, with finite man there always are. Our contingencies are as "Plan B" or other alternatives, ulterior motives and rationalizations with regards to our values, our dogmas, our societal influences, etc. over the commands of God!

God inhabits eternity. Therefore, time has no significance to Him, as a whole. However, perfect timing is crucial to God's overall plan for the ages. Scripture declares that the saint is saved by grace through faith. *(cf. Eph. 2:8,9)* But it also declares that faith is the victory that over comes the world. *(cf. 1 John 5:4)* My question is this. Since faith is the victory and not grace, why then does the traditional church place such emphasis on grace, when it is a constitutional necessity, based upon a covenant relationship? In other words, it's a given, providing that the terms and conditions of God are met! For example, an employer has provided for his employees certain provisions such as health, dental, promotion opportunities, etc. Upon hiring, each employee was given a company packet, which outlined the procedures to take advantage of the corporate provisions. However, most employees disregard these instructions and procedures. Without this knowledge of procedure, they are unable to benefit by these corporate "perks." Whose fault is that? It's not the employers fault! The fault rests entirely on the individual employees, who threw away these instructions. In doing so, they nullified and invalidated the corporate provisions which exist for their benefit. In short, they frustrated themselves, when they disre-garded the instruction and the provision! And so it is with grace! Faith then, is the procedure to validate the provisions of God's grace in our life!

Galatians 2:21 AMP
"[Therefore, I do not treat God's gracious gift as something of minor importance and defeat its very purpose]; I do not set aside and invalidate and frustrate and nullify the grace (unmerited favor) of God..."

Jesus Christ asked, "When the Son of Man cometh, shall He find faith on the earth?" *(cf. Lk. 18:8)* By this question, it is apparent that faith, as it pertains to man and his acquisition of grace, is the concern and not grace itself. Grace is eternal just as God is eternal! As stated earlier, we emphasize grace, but we neglect faith! When the denominational church neglects the procedure of faith, in effect, she throws this divine provision away. Applying this reasoning to the sixth and seventh day, it is evident that the sixth day (present) is an age of faith within the church age and the seventh day is more appropriately that age of grace! What faith is to conversion and to the future redemption of the saints of God, grace is to the manifestation of it. Let's not throw it away by disregarding the procedure!

Faith, that is counted to us as righteousness and a lifestyle of repentance are the only means which shall be our right of passage into God's rest. Once there, we no longer shall have any need for the spiritual endowments of God's grace, such as faith and repentance, because the saints of God will have ceased from their earthly labors!

Hebrews 11:6 AMP
"But without faith it is impossible to please and to be satisfactory to Him. For whoever would come near to God must [necessarily] believe that God exists and that he is a rewarder of those who earnestly and diligently seek Him."

Hebrews 12:14 AMP
"Strive to live in peace with everybody and pursue that consecration and holiness without which no one will [ever] see the Lord."

Hebrews 4:5-6
"And in this place [Kingdom of God] again, if they shall enter into my rest, seeing therefore it remaineth that some must enter therein, and they to whom it [Gospel] was first preached entered not in because of unbelief." (brackets mine)

These three verses present a condition of rest and a position of rest. Unbelief however, is disobedience, which is also rebellion. Man's *disobedience* is his rebellion against God! It carries the same attributes as rebellion and it means "to mishear, to be inattentive to, to ignore or to not heed." (Strong's Exhaustive Concordance, Greek ref. #3876 page 55)

Hebrews 4:7-10 AMP
*"Again, he sets a definite day, [a new] Today, [and gives another opportunity of securing that rest] saying through David after so long a time in the words already quoted, Today, if you would hear His voice and when you hear it, do not harden your hearts. [This mention of a rest was not a reference to their entering into Canaan.] For if Joshua had given them rest, He [God] would not speak afterward about another day. So then, there is [still] awaiting a full **and** complete Sabbath-rest reserved for the [true] people of God; **For he who has once entered [God's] rest, also has ceased from [the weariness and pain] of human labors,** just as God rested from those labors peculiarly his own."* (emphasis mine)

The Prophetic Word of Faith

Hebrews 11:1
"Now Faith is the substance of things hoped for and the evidence of things not seen."

This verse speaks of two ingredients of faith. They are substance and evidence; and the verse relates them to hope and the things not seen. This verse reminds me of two other Scriptures with the same portent as evidenced by the word, "is." They are:

Song of Songs 1:1
"The Song of songs which is Solomon's."

Revelation 19:10
"The testimony of Jesus Christ is the Spirit of Prophecy."

From a position of time or history, it appears that hope and the things not seen are future tense, while substance and evidence are past and present. So from this deduction, we learn that *the substance of faith precedes the evidence of faith*. As Song 1:1 relates, Solomon's name was *equal* to his character [song], for he was known by it. The revelation being, that the substance of things hoped for is equal to the prophetic word! The explanation is this. The Messianic Prophecies of the Old Testament, are in fact faith words [substance] spoken by the prophets who were men of faith. Since they spoke in faith, the content of their character was equal to the substance of their prophetic words. They were spirit words, spoken by spirit beings of material things hoped for. Therefore, as history and the Scriptures reveal, the prophetic word of faith spoken then, contained the very substance of the manifestation, and was therefore the evidence of future things not seen. This then made them equal! When Jesus Christ, for example, did come as prophesied, He was the embodiment and the fulfillment of the substance of hope then, but evidenced now!

Another illustration would be currency. Take a single dollar bill. The evidence of a dollar bill is obvious, because you can see it with your natural eye and hold it in your hands. Together they both affirm the truth of its existence according to reason and to life. Now let me ask you, What is it about a dollar bill that you don't see? You don't see its substance! A dollar bill is equivalent to 100 cents. One hundred cents may be further divided into two 50 cent coins, 4 quarters, 10 dimes or 20 nickels, right? So the point is this. Before you can have the evidence (dollar bill), there first must be the substance (100 cents). It's cause and effect. One must precede the other! The law of necessity demands it! You can't have the one without the other. Scriptures tell us that Abraham called those things that were not, as though they were. He understood the principles of faith to possess substance and evidence. He understood that the substance of his words had to precede the manifestation of God's grace, which was the evidence of his faith so stated.

The ingredient of faith called *substance* spoken by the prophets of the Old Testament then, was required to be spoken as prophetic words. Now that we are in the New Testament, the ingredient of faith called *evidence* now, is the testimony of Jesus Christ, as the Word made flesh, which must be accepted as the only way to heaven, for He is the prophesied Messiah, Who is full of grace and truth! In the same manner, when you consider the seals and trumpets which contain the wrath of God spoken of in Revelations, chapters 6 -9, that have yet to be opened and sounded upon impenitent humanity, there does exist a connection between faith, repentance and prophecy. The connection being, that the substance of the written Word of God, as spoken and recorded in antiquity now documented, shall soon present the evidence, fulfillment and the reality of such prophetic words then. Therefore, faith, repentance and prophecy are uniquely related!

There's a Warrant Out for Your Arrest!

There's a warrant out for your arrest! The Supreme Court of heaven has issued a bench warrant for all of fallen humanity! This warrant has a dual purpose. First, it's a search (inspection) warrant as well as an order for our incarceration! Look at Saul of Tarsus. A Pharisee, trained under the tutelage of Gamiel. He was highly educated and highly dangerous! As a terrorist, Saul embarked on a journey to Damascus with letters to further persecute the saints. In this capacity, Saul was, at the very least, an accomplice to murder and mayhem! As far as God was concerned, he was a felon and therefore a fugitive! While traveling, on the road to Damascus, he was arrested by the Judge of the universe, Jesus Christ! Since Saul was arrested, he was also apprehended. Having been pulled over, and in the presence of the Almighty, Saul was immediately deprived of his liberties and freedoms of his carnality and of the world system of which he was a part. Saul, was then incarcerated and suddenly he became a prisoner of the Judge. It's important to know that Saul did not resist arrest. Neither did he evade arrest as is the normal reaction of violators and criminals. Neither did he stagger! Rather, he submitted himself to the authority of Jesus Christ as Scripture relates. Saul, who was a terrorist before his conversion, later became known as Paul, the Apostle to the Gentiles. As a prisoner of the Lord his God, He labored to enter into God's rest through faith and repentance. Paul learned to reconcile his soul to God, by obeying the incarceration instructions provided him by Almighty God. He preached the kingdom of God from these terms and conditions of God's Word.

Paul literally wore [bore] his prison uniform on his body! Like the striped garment issued to any inmate, Paul's uniform, were the scars and stripes, wounds and other injuries which he endured. These marks of persecution, were etched into his flesh and upon his heart for the remainder of his life! He became a dead man walking, because for him to live was Christ and to die was gain!

Galatians 2:20
"For I am crucifies with Christ, nevertheless, I live; yet not I, but Christ liveth within me: and the life which I now live in the flesh, I live by the faith of the Son of God, who loved me, and gave himself for me." (cf. Acts 9:1-9; Gal. 6:17; Phile. 1)

The Call of Repentance

As you read this investigation of repentance, you will plant seeds of repentance into your heart, because repentance causes you to be planted! **Truth #1: The call to repentance is a sound of alarm declaring you to change, while the call of repentance is a challenge to renew the spirit of your mind and then to change!**

This investigation of repentance shall teach you that the power of the cross fuels the call, for it is the power of God unto salvation; and thus far has been a collection of several theological concepts on or about faith, grace and repentance beneath the surface level of understanding, which merely converts the sinner. **Truth #2: If all we ever hear is repentance at the conversion level, for the sake of the sinner soon to be sainted, then the rest of the corporate Body of Christ suffers, as this will be all they will ever learn. Repentance then, must be the foundation for revival, personally and corporately!** The Body of Christ must wake up to the truth that without repentance, revival cannot exist and that we are not just sinners who are saved by grace! Rather, we are also saints who are saved through faith!

Ephesians 2:8a AMP
"For it is by free grace (God's unmerited favor) that you are saved, delivered from judgment and made partakers of Christ's salvation through [your] faith..."

2 Peter 1:9 AMP
"[At the same time] you received the result (outcome, consummation) of your faith, the salvation of your souls."

1 John 5:4 AMP
"For whatsoever is born of God is victorious over the world; and this is the victory that conquers the world, even our faith."

An Elementary Presumption

The worldly church has an elementary presumption about repentance from dead works for the remission of sins. However good the intentions, this presumptive dogma will never lead to spiritual maturity, because there is no emphasis on repentance as that which cultivates salvation, or faith beyond the surface renderings. Trying to be saved without specific knowledge is a waste of time. What's more, this ignorance is carnality! You see, God desires his people to be zealous! He expects us to pursue it, to master it, to be skillful with it and to live it! This investigation will provide the insight, the depth and specific knowledge as revealed from the very heart of God! These "Truths of Repentance" shall lead you towards spiritual maturity, facilitating growth in grace and knowledge. You will slaughter a sacred cow. That bovine being, your carnality as that residue of sin!

The Presumptive Heritage of the Church

The laws of interpretation and language demand that a mutual agreement of terms be established to promote understanding of any subject or topic. When there is a violation of these laws, confusion, disorder and dissension exist. What I am about to say will most likely and in all probability be of great offense to some and of great delight to others, for a *sacred cow* is about to be slaughtered! The dogma of "Once saved, Always saved," is this black heifer! You won't find it in any document, but it is nevertheless a misrepresentation of Scripture. It is a presumptuous heritage, whose liberality remains a reckless sin to the Body of Christ! The traditional church must recognize that this deceptive dogma is piecemeal theology and she must repent of this abuse of scriptural interpretation, for it is an iniquity of the carnal mind and a violation against the laws of God!

As any butcher would use specific knives to properly cleave animal meat, so too must the Church use specific knives to cut and to sever truth from deceit. For the Body of Christ, that blade is specific knowledge of the Word of God, for it is sharper than any two edged sword. *(cf. Heb. 4:12)* For the purpose of this butchering, it is necessary to come to a mutual understanding, for the laws of language and interpretation demand it. Otherwise, confusion and division shall remain. Therefore, the following definitions and scriptural support are provided to convey this intent. These definitions were obtained from the Webster"s Dictionary. I have also provided examples as I felt I should.

Presuppose: 1. To suppose or to assume beforehand; take for granted. 2. To require or imply as a preceding condition, presumptive: based on a probability, giving reasonable grounds for belief, presumptive, circumstantial evidence.

For instance, revival is necessary, because of a back sliding church. The fact that the traditional church has regressed into carnality, mandates that revival occur. Another example would be the purpose for the shovel, which exist by reason of the dirt. If there was no dirt, then there would be no need for the shovel! But because there is dirt, the shovel is necessary.

Presumptuous: 1. Too bold or forward; taking too much for granted, showing over confidence, arrogance or effrontery.

Heritage: 1. Property that is or can be inherited. 2. a) Something handed down from one's ancestors or the past, as a characteristic, a culture, tradition, etc... b) The rights, burdens, or status resulting from being born in a certain time or place, birthright.

Heritage: (synonym) The most general of these words applies either to property passed down to an heir, or a tradition, culture, etc..., passed on to a later generation such as our heritage of freedom.

There is a sin of ignorance! However, ignorance is not the same as presumption. Ignorance tends towards possessing no ability to learn, due to circumstances beyond one's control. Whereas, presumption is a predominant mind set perpetrated by choice! This then makes choice to be an act or function of the will. *(cf. Lev. 4:1-4; Num. 15:28-31)*

Moses, in Deuteronomy 6, exhorted the Hebrew nation with strong urging and warnings to hear [listen and receive] God and to keep the Ten Commandments which required them to love God with their whole heart, soul and *might*. I emphasize might, because by definition, it implies a lessor degree of probability of man's obligation to comply with the terms and conditions of God's Word. Moses said that they were not to tempt the Lord God with their presumptuous mind sets. But Scripture shows that they did many times over. Moses also instructed the people to teach their children the [heritage] in the Ten Commandments of the Lord their God. *(cf. Deut. 6:1-25)* And yet we know, according to Scripture, that this was not done, generationally.

Scripture also states that in the passage of time, God shall raise up a Prophet like unto Moses and the words that this Prophet shall speak shall be the Word of God. Conversely, the presumptive words spoken by false prophets, shall fall to the ground like trash in a gutter and the false prophet shall die! *(cf. Deut. 18:15-22)*

Deuteronomy 1:43
"So I spake unto you and you would not hear, but rebelled against the commandment of the Lord and went presumptuously up the hill."

Psalm 19:13
"Keep back thy servant also from presumptuous sins; let them not have dominion over me: then shall I be upright and I shall be innocent from the great transgression."

1 Corinthians 10:6-11
"Neither let us tempt Christ as some of them have tempted, and were destroyed of serpents." (cf. Num. 21:6-7)

As long as the carnal church misinterprets God's Word or is disobedient to it, she might as well participate in a lynching, because she will only hang herself out to dry! Moreover, as long as people live out their lives in their carnality, they too will hand out rope to hang themselves, for as long as they loiter around in their presumptuous lifestyle, they tighten the noose around their necks, all because they choose to be stubborn and remain obstinately disobedient! As to this sacred cow, it's my intent to further disembowel this influential dogma through this inquest; but for now, this should make you aware of the falsity of this carnality.

Doing Time with Three Hots and a Cot

A *penitentiary* is the modern incarceration facility and is either a Federal or State institution with roots that date back in antiquity. It was here, that the convict occupied a *cell of penitence*. In his cell, the *convict* was to *reconcile* his ways back to God and society. Presently, for the less serious criminal, there also exists the municipal jail and the state youth authorities for the juvenile offenders.

Convicts, whether they like it or not or realize it or not, live a lifestyle of penitence! The duration of their sentence requires them to reside behind bars, in their cell of penitence and as a matter of routine, every convict is afforded a Bible. The very word, *penitent* means "to repent, to be willing to atone for." Since penitent is a singular expression, then repentance is the repetition of being penitent and this speaks of a lifestyle of repentance. In this investigation, you will learn what exactly God is telling the denominational church about repentance. Almighty God is waiting for her to come to grips with the fact that she has *evaded* and *resisted* arrest! Like the criminal or fugitive who, as a man on the run, has committed the most serious of crimes against society, the wayward church must not bypass salvation any longer by rejecting the full counsel of God's Word. Nor continue to give priority to the doctrines and dogmas of men. *(cf. Mark 7: 8-9, 13)* The Body of Christ and humanity as a whole, had better agree with God's Word quickly, taking His sober advice. **Truth #3: A lifestyle of repentance means to agree with our adversary quickly, while we are in the way with him; lest at anytime our adversary deliver us to the Judge and the Judge deliver us to the officer and we be cast into prison.** *(cf. Mat. 5:25)*

A Prisoner of Jesus Christ

As long as people remain in their carnality and befriend the things of this world, hostility shall exist between impenitent humanity and God! Almighty God requires accountability and just as any convict is a prisoner who is held accountable for his actions against society, likewise, the saints of God are obligated to live accountably before their God! The Apostle Paul, provided to the Church, his perspective from the position of a prisoner. Paul stated, *"I am a prisoner of Jesus Christ!"* *(cf. Eph. 3:1, 4:1; Phile. 1)* He implied, as the Apostle to the Gentile nations, that the Church must also do her time, as a prisoner. Paul said, that he was apprehended! Literally, Paul self-sentenced himself! He yielded his earthen vessel, voluntarily! He recognized that he was spiritually bankrupt, and that he could not afford the cost of his carnality. Shouldn't the Bride of Christ yield her vessel as well, following Paul's example before the Judge of the universe seizes embezzled or stolen property as evidence? For as long as people remain carnal, they are that embezzled or stolen property! Throughout his new life in God, Paul became a dead man walking! **Truth #4: To self-sentence one's self is to adopt a lifestyle of repentance!**

Notes:

Chapter 2
Theological Concepts and Ideas

He Shall Sever and His Wrath Shall Fall

Genesis 6:1
"And it came to pass, when men began to multiply on the face of the earth, and daughters were born unto them,"

Here in Genesis 6:1 we read, *"And it came to pass..."* This phrase denotes an unspecified passage of time, be it hours, days, weeks, months, years, decades or centuries. It applies to the activity of all men, during their life time, which God observes and He addresses during this time of passage in the history of humanity. Almighty God alerts each of us to the truth that He shall sever and His wrath and judgment shall fall upon impenitent humanity! *(cf. Is. 26:9-10; Rev. 6:17; Jude 4-7)*

Genesis 6:3a
"And the Lord said, My spirit shall not always strive with man..."

Here's a question for you. How does God strive with man? He does so through His forbearance and long suffering. But of what? God's tolerance with man's carnality is the answer and this is unequivocally evident throughout Scripture. But just what is meant by the word, *strive* and what are its ramifications? *Strive* means, "to rule, to judge (as an umpire) as at law, to contend, execute judgment, minister judgment, plead (the cause of), at strife, strive." (Strong's Exhaustive Concordance, Heb. ref. #1777, page 30) So from a historical time line, what Almighty God stated in Genesis 6 about man's wickedness, has been clear throughout history. However, in these closing days of the times of the gentiles, we must realize that our time is very short and that God's forbearance and long suffering are limited to His providential time line. As shall be shown throughout this work, repentance is the judgment of God's forbearance, for it is the inspiration of the doctrine of God. Specifically as it is related in Romans 2:4-5.

Romans 2:4-5 AMP
"Or are you [so blind as to] trifle with and presume upon and despise and underestimate the wealth of His kindness and forbearance and long suffering patience? Are you unmindful or actually ignorant [of the fact] that God's kindness is intended to lead you to repent (to change your mind and inner man to accept God's will)? But by your callous stubbornness and impenitence of heart you are storing up wrath and indignation for yourself on the day of wrath and indignation, when God's righteous judgment (just doom) will be revealed."

Isaiah 42:14
"I have long time holden my peace; I have been still, and refrained myself: now will I cry like a travailing woman; I will destroy and devour at once."

Psalm 103:9
"He will not always chide: neither will He keep His anger forever."

Isaiah 26:9-10
"..for when thy judgments are in the earth, the inhabitants of

the world will learn righteousness. Let favour be shewed to the wicked, yet will he not learn righteousness..."

In Psalm 103 verse 9, the word *chide* means, "to hold a controversy, complain, rebuke, admonish, to scold now, to reprove mildly." (Strong's Exhaustive Concordance Heb. #7378, page 108) Could it be that Almighty God is articulating to humanity today that time, as we know it, is so very short that no longer will He mildly reprove humanity for our wickedness and that more severe corrective measures await us? I guess some people must learn the hard way, if they learn anything at all. It's been said of the Holy Spirit that He is a gentleman. However, keeping with the above definition, it appears then, that God will no longer present Himself as gentle to impenitent humanity, neither will He mildly chasten us for all of the observed carnality of men. Therefore, a change of heart must occur within us! Almighty God shall not alter His plan just to satisfy the inconsistencies of fallen humanity!

2 Timothy 3:15-17 AMP
*"And how from your childhood you have had a knowledge of and been acquainted with the sacred Writings, which are able to **instruct** you and give you the **understanding for salvation** which comes through faith in Christ Jesus [through the leaning of the entire human personality on God in Christ Jesus in absolute trust and confidence in His power, wisdom, and good-ness]. Every Scripture is God-breathed (given by His inspiration) and profitable for instruction, for reproof, and conviction of sin, for correction of error and discipline **in obedience**, [and] **for training in righteousness** (in holy living, in conformity to God's will in thought, purpose, and action), So that the man of God may be complete and proficient, well fitted and throughly equipped for every good work."* (emphasis mine)

Anything may become a source of heartache or frustration. Eventually, this contention could lead to an ultimatum, and the option presented may vary. So, to sever yourself from the source of frustration often requires drastic changes in locality or relationships, and this always involves individuals, circumstances, even political and spiritual associations. Man's wickedness has also become a frustration to God, and left unchecked, His frustration shall build to contention, just as it does between people. But how does a man cease from his striving with God? **Truth #5: He ceases from striving by cutting, severing or removing himself from the source of misery or frustration or change the environment in which he may live or work!** In other words, he no longer will make provision for the flesh.

Genesis 6:5
"And God saw that the wickedness of man was great in the earth, and that every imagination of the thoughts of his heart was evil continually."

In Genesis 6:5 we read that Almighty God observed that the wickedness of men was great upon the face of the earth. Couple this with verse 1, *"And it came to pass..."*, and it should be evident to you that their wickedness spoke of a carnal lifestyle, because wickedness appeared in the ways and schemes of men, even in their thoughts and imaginations. Although times change, people by design, really don't. As it was for these souls then, so it remains for humanity today, that carnal tendencies are lodged within the soul of every man and these define the conduct and behavior [character] of all as being constitutionally sinful. *(cf. Psa. 51:5)* These self-indulgent works of the flesh, are the outward displays and expressions of the carnality that resides within the unregenerate soul of man! We must remember that the soul of man is unseen, and yet his character, which issues from within his soul, is outwardly expressed!

Genesis 6:6-7
"And it [evil deeds, wickedness] repented [regretted] the Lord that He had made man on the face of the earth and it grieved Him at His heart... I will destroy man whom I have created from the face of the earth... for it [man's wickedness] repented me that I had made them." (brackets mine)

Twice within these verses, the word, *repent* is written for the very first time in the scriptural text. This implies that since Almighty God spoke it, then His word is settled in heaven and forever. *(cf. Psa. 119:89)* Therefore His Word of repentance is also legislated for man! These verses denote man's wickedness and how it effects and infects everything. The landscape, the air we breathe, the plant and animal life, and the fish and insects are all contaminated by man's carnality! It's for this reason that heaven and earth shall flee from the presence of Almighty God, for they shall find no place of repentance. *(cf. Rev. 20:11)* Of specific note, is the fact that repentance has a place! Although it may not be a physical locality, such as your personal address, just the same it does have a place. That place is intended to be within man's soul and is probably more akin to a position in God as in a destination towards Him. *(cf. Acts 20:21; Rev. 20:11; Heb. 12:17)* Man's carnality then, causes God to regret man's sin! His regret is to our disgrace because of the carnality of impenitent humanity! **Truth #6: The place of repentance is intended to be within the soul of man. It is for this reason why Almighty God gave it to us!**

God Shall Set His Face Against the Crookedness of Man

The Bible teaches that Almighty God shall set His face against the froward [crookedness] activity of men! Why? Because man has arrogantly set up idols within his heart and has placed these stumbling blocks of his iniquity before the face of God!

Ezekiel 15:7
"And I will set my face against them...and ye shall know that I am the Lord, when I set my face against them."

Deuteronomy 7:10
"And repayeth them that hate Him to their face, to destroy them: he will not be slack to him that hateth him, he will repay him to his face."

Whenever a man flaunts his wickedness to another, that observed behavior is at the same time, set before the face of another. It's similar to the inconsiderate smoker, who shows no regard for the air space of others and smokes anyway, just because he can. As it was then, so it remains today, that mankind has set the stumbling block of his carnality before his own face, the face of another, and the face of Almighty God! These character flaws have desecrated the face of the entire earth, her waters and have even polluted the atmospheres of heaven.

The Evidence Speaks for Itself

Jeremiah 3:2b
"...and thou hast polluted the land with thy whoredoms and with thy wickedness."

The Prophet Jeremiah, lived approximately six hundred thirty years before Christ. As he addressed the people (men and women alike) he said that their whoredoms and their wickedness polluted the land. Today, in the year 2003, it is common knowledge that the entire planet, which includes her water ways and its atmospheres, are even more polluted. Forget the spiritual intention here; but strictly from an evidentiary position, the facts are that mankind has trashed this planet and everything in it! Whereas, the carnality of the people in Jeremiah's day polluted the land, how much more so today has the carnality of man trashed this entire planet! The evidence supports this crime of humanity, and it's everywhere! If you still need concrete evidence, just drink your filthy water, inhale the petroleum laden air, and consume chemically laced foods. The Law of Necessity stipulates that for every event or act of the will, there are sequences of causes or determinations that produce an effect. (Webster's) Therefore, the causative factor, as pertaining to Jeremiah, has been man's carnality (whoredoms, wickedness) then, and the determination of man's carnality now, is the effect of the pollution of planet earth! **Truth #7: Whereas, the evidence [pollution] of the effects of man's carnality is clearly seen and known all around, it's only a reflection of the objective symptoms of man's wretchedness within!**

In some countries abroad, the traveling United States citizen is still known as the "Ugly American." This expression connotes that Americans are wasteful and perhaps superfluous with the excesses of life of which they are stewards. Abroad, Americans are seen as those who brandish their opulence. To other nations, America flaunts her power and influence. Similarly, we Americans regard foreigners as being something different or even lacking in their mental perceptions or quality of life. Even our own history supports this fact when you consider the racial tensions of our society today, the hostilities that existed between the native American and the white settlers of yesteryear and the societal influence of the "carpet-baggers" and plantation owners and the slaves! Since superficial differences and bigotries are realities for all peoples, they do portray a symptom of carnality that is common before the face of each other and the face of God!

Did God?

Did God actually state in Genesis 6:6-7 that He hates all of mankind, whom He created in the very image or impression of Himself? *(cf. Gen.1:26-28, 2:7)* If this were the case, then the Hebrews, who were just delivered from Egyptian bondage, were correct when they murmured against Moses that God had taken them out to the desert just to slay them. *(cf. Ex.14:10-12)*

Did God imply that He hates Himself or whatever imperfections of Himself that He might see in His creation, man? I answer, No! Because God so loved the world, He gave His only begotten Son, for why should He send His Son Jesus Christ to die for a creation that He hates? *(cf. John 3:16; Gen. 3:19)* Can Almighty God, Who is Love, defile His own nature and hate man? Again, the answer is, No! Although He truly loves man, He does hate the wickedness within the carnal soul of man! Did God consider Himself a failure when He observed the deficiencies and wickedness of humanity? No! God is not a failure, neither did He create junk! Man however, has literally trashed all that God did create on, about and within the earth! Although the earth and the air we breathe are still suitable to support life, it must be remembered that with all its tainted beauty, nature's beauty is only a dimmed reflection of what it once was, and glimpses of what it shall become again! *(cf. Jer. 2:7-3:2; Rev. 21:1)*

We Must Regret Our Evil Activity

Have you ever regretted [repented, mourned] a bad decision, a spoken word, or a particular wrong deed, even though it seemed to be the right thing to do or it seemed convenient or expedient at the time? Of course you have. Genesis 6:6-7 for example, speaks of man's carnality and God's hatred of it. Yet these verses state that God repented, that is, He regretted the activity of corrupt humanity. Shouldn't we then, also regret our own carnality just as God? **Truth #8: A lifestyle of repentance requires**

that we possess a remorsefulness and a deep regret for all our carnality, so much so, that it grieves our heart! In other words, repentance must be an experience and a revelation!

Look at it this way. As any illness or injury would often effect one's entire disposition, emotional state, attitude, and mental processes, repentance too must also affect our living and afflict our soul! Without this, true, godly repentance must remain suspect. Merely stating, "I have sinned," or "I am a sinner." is not enough, because without repentance, of this import, there is no corresponding action to faith! **Truth #9: Therefore, a lifestyle of repentance is that corresponding action to faith, for it is a work of righteousness!** *(cf. James 2:14-26)*

2 Corinthians 7:9-10 AMP
*"Yet I am glad now, not because you were **pained**, but because you were **pained into repentance** [and so turned back to God]: for you **felt a grief such as God meant for you to feel**... for godly grief and the pain that **God is permitted to direct** produce [in you] a repentance that leads to and contributes to salvation and deliverance from evil, and it never brings regret..."* (emphasis mine)

These verses teach that there are certain conditions which any person must meet to experience godly repentance of this import. **Truth #10: First, a lifestyle of repentance will cause a pain of heart. Like a wound that has been exposed to iodine, or a transplanted tree that has experienced root shock, repentance will expose deep rooted carnality, as that residue of sin within the soul, for the entrance of God's word brings light. Secondly, a lifestyle of repentance produces grief. This is not just to feel sorry for yourself, just because you were caught, but it intimates a genuine abhorrence for your carnality that still resides within. Thirdly, a lifestyle of repentance means that God is permitted to direct whatever purging needs to be achieved and**

in whatever manner! Having met all three conditions, salvation is guaranteed, for in and through repentance, salvation is cultivated! *(cf. Phil. 2:12)*

> *Mark 5:29*
> *"And straightway the fountain of her blood was dried up; and she felt in her body that she had been healed of that plague."*

The woman with the issue of blood, as referred to in the verse above, felt healing virtue enter into her and heal her body! It is evident that without faith, she would not and could not have received her healing. Repentance is no different, because a lifestyle of repentance provides healing for the soul, which leads to salvation! **Truth #11: Whereas, faith affords tangible cures, a lifestyle of repentance provides intangible remedies for the soul unto salvation! Since faith is substance and evidence, repentance then is the cleansing agent of the soul!** They are of equal importance, because faith and repentance are as the handshake of two intelligent people who have entered a covenant agreement between them. Otherwise, there remains only a gesture of friendship, gone unheeded. *(cf. Prov. 1:24, 11:21, 16:6; Acts 20:21)*

But I must also state that without faith, there is no need for repentance. Therefore, I stipulate that this woman had received a revelation of true, godly repentance that was equal with her faith to be healed! It stands to reason then, that repentance can and should be experienced even as faith! This experience of repentance is something we do based upon a personal revelation. **Truth #12: Whereas, a confession of faith corresponds to our countenance, a lifestyle of repentance conforms to our carnality!** This lifestyle of repentance is addressed in another way, as found in Joel 2:13. In part, this verse reads, *"...to rend our hearts and not our garments..."* The word *rend* means, "to tear out with violence." This implies a deep hatred for evil of any sort or origin, that still resides within the soul. Again, a lifestyle of repentance is something that you must experience and then develop, because the blessings at this degree of penitence, regurgitates man's carnality!

A Lemon is not a Make of an Automobile

God loves humanity, His created spiritual image of Himself! However, He does possess a righteous displeasure and indignation for the disgusting, detestable and the deplorable ways and doings of every person. As an illustration, consider the purchase of an automobile. Due to mechanical or electrical discrepancies, you as the owner, take your vehicle back to the mechanic for repair. You instinctively know that the mechanic won't destroy the basic concept or design of your vehicle, but you also know that he will make the necessary adjustments, or modifications and take the corrective measures as required. These corrective methods are still based upon the basic design and so it shall be with humanity. Almighty God wants us to know that He recognizes the sin problem as a distinct issue/entity within us, individually. However, we must also know that if we refuse to accept the corrective measure provided, to repair the carnality within our soul through a lifestyle of repentance, then God will destroy the sin problem first, but take us along with it, because as far as He is concerned, we and the sin problem have become one! Although God does understand the reasons why, does not mean too say that He condones a carnal lifestyle! Therefore, should a person continue in his corruption or allows it to remain, then he shall reap that same corruption in the end. It must also be remembered that faith is not a reward for a scant interest in our Blessed Savior. Faith is the soul's adhesive that binds two together. Faith then must be the mutual union of two intelligent beings, and in this case, God and man.

Galatians 6:7-8
"Be not deceived; God is not mocked: for whatsoever a man soweth, that shall he also reap. For he that soweth to his flesh shall of the flesh reap corruption; but he that soweth to the Spirit shall of the Spirit reap life everlasting."

Noah Found Grace

Genesis 6:8 basically states that Noah found grace in the eyes of the Lord. If God hates man, as some suppose, why then did Noah find grace with Almighty God? Noah found grace, because he was a just man (verse 9) and perfect in his generation. Noah walked with God, where the others chose not to. A lifestyle of repentance then precipitates God's grace! **Truth #13: A lifestyle of repentance mandates that everything about our lives agree with God's instructions of holiness and righteousness, because left to ourselves, man's goodness is always base and inferior in quality and content!** Furthermore, a lifestyle of repentance is a charge that is directed towards our conduct and behavior, in that we are to be righteous, even as He is righteous! (*cf. Psa. 66:18, 81:13, 95:10, 139:17; Is. 1:1-13, 55:6-9; Jer. 29:11; Micah 3:4; Heb. 3:10*)

John 6:63
"It is the spirit that quickeneth; the flesh profits nothing: the words that I speak unto you, they are spirit and they are life."

This verse intimates that the obscurity of man's goodness and morality are nothing more than a fleeting suggestion of his self righteousness. After all, even a criminal may be kind and loving to his own and yet, could also be on the most wanted list!

One Choice is No Choice

Suppose for example, that Almighty God presented His

Word to other peoples of the ancient world, only to be rejected by them. Now suppose that only the Hebrew nation accepted God and His Word and through Abraham, they became God's chosen people. Should this supposition be correct, then God is calling out to each new generation and to every man, however He knows that most will not answer. *(cf. 1 Pet. 1:2)* He has extended His mighty hand down to all mankind, but most have chosen to disregard it. So it is evident that God, Who is no respecter of persons, has presented His Word to all of mankind, but only a few will respond favorably to His call and take His hand into theirs. **Truth #14: A lifestyle of repentance then, is the manifestation of righteousness wherein, God's people are recipients of His favor and grace!**

Repentance as a Memorial

How soon do people forget. It's been said that if men forget the mistakes of the past, they are bound to repeat them again. **Truth #15: A lifestyle of repentance serves as a memorial to the ever present carnality of man!** In support of this, I remind you of the Hebrew Passover, which was a memorial of their deliverance from Egyptian bondage then and which still remains today; and the woman with the alabaster box, whom Christ said in essence, would be a memorial to her as long as The Gospel is preached. *(cf. Ex. 12:12-14; Matt. 26:6-13)* But more will be said of this later.

Notes:

Chapter 3

Repentance in the Book of Exodus

Exodus 13:17
"And it came to pass, when Pharaoh had let the people go, that God led them not through the way of the land of the Philistines, although, that was near; for God said, Lest peradventure the people repent when they see war, and they return to Egypt:"

Freedom From Bondage

"And it came to pass..." There's that phrase again. It denotes an unspecified passage of time. Take for example, the movie, The Ten Commandments. This film is a 3 hour 28 minute motion picture in which time compression is used and as such, it is Hollywood's rendition of God's intervention, in the abbreviated sense. Yet verse 17 states, *"And it came to pass..."* Again, this phrase pertains to the history of man's conduct and behavior as it pertains to his carnality and his ungodly character. So why didn't God lead the people through the land of the Philistines since it was so near? The reason was that four hundred years of Egyptian incarceration incapacitated them physically and institutionalized the Hebrew nation psychologically, rendering them unfit for battle. This Egyptian torment dispossessed the Hebrews, and stripped them of their dignity, integrity and identity. In this diminished capacity, Almighty God knew that the Hebrew people were as grasshoppers and were in no condition to wage war. Interestingly, the word, *torment* means "pun-

ish, punishment, grasshopper, to self sentence one's self, to wrap one's self in the head with the fist." (Strong's Exhaustive Concordance Greek text, ref.# 2849, 2851, 2852, page 43; *cf. Num. 13:28-33; 1 John 4:18*)

The Violent Take It by Force

To wage war or do battle requires spiritual, mental and physical training. Whereas, any abusive environment, relationship or situation disrobes the victim of dignity, integrity and identity, such conditioning is then necessary to reacquire lost vision and the accompanying aspirations which necessitate it. Without this conditioning, the victim becomes or remains a beaten, down trodden, inanimate object, just as the Hebrews were. They were invalids, spiritually, physically, psychologically and emotionally. As in Genesis 6:3, there must be a severing, which such conditioning would provide. Severing often involves isolation. This isolation is often a wilderness experience that challenges comfort zones. Like water that seeks the path of least resistance, the unregenerate, unre-newed, carnal mind seeks the path of minimum restraint, because that which is familiar is the path of least resistance!

It's a matter of authority and a proper attitude determines which. Because slavery dishonors labor, it introduces to the victim distress, oppression and ignorance, but to the taskmaster, it acquaints him with idleness, pride and luxury and always at the expense of others, who are more subservient. Therefore, we are either in authority or we are under the authority of, and impulsive decisions made, based solely upon emotion, ulterior motives or convenience, are choices made for that which is familiar. Whereas, the law of sin (carnality) within our soul has a law or rule over our selfish propensities, so too does the law of the Spirit of life in Christ Jesus have a rule, as an expressed judgment of God, for it is the true path of expediency as that way which leads towards eternal life! But the Hebrew people decided that life in bondage was more suitable to them than to risk hazarding their lives on that which was unfamiliar. **Truth#16: A lifestyle of repentance means freedom; regret, based solely upon emotions, ulterior motives or convenience, means bondage, again!**

This is applicable individually, as well as to the national and international affairs of men. *(cf. Ex. 14:10-12; Deut. 8:1-3)*

Repentance at the Tabernacle

Exodus 26:7, 12-14

*"And thou shalt make curtains of **goats hair** to be **a covering upon the tabernacle:** eleven curtains shalt thou make...And the remnant that remaineth of the curtains of the tent, the half curtain that remaineth, shall hang over the backside of the tabernacle. And a cubit on the one side and a cubit on the other side of that which remaineth in the length of the curtains of the tent, it shall hang over the sides of the tabernacle on this side and on that side, to cover it. And thou shalt make a covering for the tent of rams' skins dyed red, and a covering above of badgers' skins." (cf. Ex. 36:14; Num. 31:20)* (emphasis mine)

In verse 7, we learn that eleven curtains were made of goat's hair and not skin. These curtains were most likely made of the same material as sackcloth which eventually each person probably owned as a covering for themselves. This premise is based on the fact that other natural resources such as hemp, jute, twine, rope or fabrics were scarcely to be found in the desert, too say the least. Consequently, the sackcloth used, was to become emblematic of the tabernacle curtains! These curtains were woven on a weaving machine called a warp, as was probably the sackcloth. *(cf. Lev. 13:49)* In verses 12-14 above, we also learn that the tabernacle was covered by these curtains. The spiritual significance being that Almighty God is fully aware of man's carnality as that residue of sin, for he remembered Adam and

Eve's disobedience. He remembered the two murders by Cain and by his grandson, La'mech. *(cf. Gen. 4:8, 23)* He remembered the wickedness of all humanity and how this wickedness caused the flood to cover the entire planet! He remembered how, left to themselves after the flood, mankind's carnality and disobedience in the land of Shi'nar, continued to wreak havoc within the soul of all men.

Therefore, as a memorial to how things once were before the fall, and of how things shall become once again, Almighty God validated man's carnality through repentance, which would be God's statute of reconciliation between man's soul and Himself. *(cf. 2 Cor. 5:18-19)* Furthermore, Almighty God stipulated that each curtain would drape the tabernacle by one cubit. The implication being that God has placed a limit or boundary on the carnality of men, for He knows that left alone, man's carnality would categorically destroy everything in heaven and on earth. He therefore, substantiated repentance as His doctrine which was to be man's perpetual obligation!

A Tabernacle, Temple or a Shrine

A shrine is a secret place within a place. Like the kingdom of heaven exists within the Kingdom of God or as a closet is within a room of any house, similarly a shrine is located within a temple. Therefore, what the tabernacle was to the Old Testament, as the tent of God within the Hebrew encampment, the saints of God, in the New Testament are His temple of the New Testament Church and their hearts are to become His shrine. *(cf. 1 Cor. 6:19-20)* Consequently, this exterior temple/body has within it a shrine [heart], that secret place which is especially set apart as a closet to arouse devotion to God. *(cf. Mat. 6:6; Luke 12:2-3)* **Truth #17: So then, a true "shriner" is that saintly temple whose perfect heart is that secret dwelling place within his soul, and through a lifestyle of repentance, he has access to**

God, for without holiness no man shall see God! *(cf. Psa. 101:2; Heb.3:6: Heb. 12:14)*

Types and Shadows

Each animal sacrificed was a type and shadow of Jesus Christ and of His blood shed on Calvary's hill. The Mercy seat also portrayed Jesus Christ as our blessed Redeemer and Propitiation through faith in His blood. Remarkably, the tabernacle curtains were also a type and shadow of the outward display of repentance as that doctrine of God, which reflects the contrite (crushed, powdered, bruised) heart of God and that of every saint given to repentance! Even the sanctuary utensils and vessels were covered with goat's hair! (cf. Num. 4:5-15) Why? Because each item covered, represents for the saint, each and every aspect of his carnality within the deep, undiscovered caverns of his soul. Moreover, the tabernacle curtains were a type and shadow of what God required as the only means of salvation namely; bloodshed for the remission (pardon, deliverance, forgiveness, liberty) of sins, that residue of which is man's carnality. We must remember that what we don't uncover God shall not cover. These curtains of sackcloth typified the flood which covered the earth as well as symbolized the blood covering of Jesus Christ, *for God so loved the world that He gave His only begotten Son! (cf. John 3:16)* In this sense, these curtains were as a pall that is commonly used to drape or cover a coffin. **Truth #18: A lifestyle of repentance is therefore, a curtain of God's sanctifying grace and the saints covering and consecration to God!** *(cf. 1 Pet. 1:2)*

Repentance as the Knowledge of Salvation

God taught Moses all the specifics of the tabernacle including its construction, the materials required, the priestly garments, the curtains, the utensils and vessels, etc. Moses then taught Aaron, Aaron's sons and the Hebrew people. Surely, this knowledge of God was a revelation to Moses! Such revelation was an unveiling of divine mysteries to Moses and all the people! Almighty God gave it to Moses so that he would disclose and make known to the people the pattern of that which already existed in heaven. Interestingly, the book of Revelation repeats this descent of divine revelation and therefore, supports this postulation which is made.

Revelation 1:1-2
"The Revelation of Jesus Christ, which **God** *gave unto* **him***, to shew unto his* **servants** *things which must shortly come to pass; and he sent and signified it by his angel unto his* **servant** *John: Who bare record of the word of God, and the testimony of Jesus Christ, and of all things that he saw." (cf. Heb. 8:1-5)* (emphasis mine)

The book of Revelation teaches that Jesus Christ shall be revealed to a corrupt people who have populated an unrighteous earth. Here in Exodus, however, God has revealed Himself, His statutes and precepts to a stiff-necked people who have also populated an unrighteous earth. All things being equal, this revelation [knowledge] was to be taught to one and all so that every person would see what is the fellowship of the mystery of Christ, which from the beginning of the world has been hid in God. Therefore, in this regard, repentance is not only the doctrine of God, but it is also the knowledge of salvation! *(cf. Eph. 1:9-18; 3:9; 2 Pet. 3:9, 11, 13-14)* It must be stated that faith, although not specifically mentioned as yet, was practiced by the people, for without faith there would be no need to repent. *(cf. 1 John 3:7; 5:17)* **Truth #19: Therefore, the knowledge of salvation facilitates God's righteousness in and through a lifestyle of repentance!**

The Urim and Thummin

Exodus 28:30

"And thou shalt put in the breastplate of judgment the Urim and the Thummin; and they shall be upon Aaron's heart, when he goeth in before the Lord: and Aaron shall bear the judgment of the children of Israel upon his heart before the Lord continually."

This verse describes the manner of dress for the high priest, Aaron. Strict adherence to this dress code was mandatory! Specifically, the preceding two verses specify that the golden ephod and the breastplate of judgment were to be worn together. These items were never to be worn separately when donned by the high priest. But what is their significance? The ephod was a garment worn for service and ministry at the altar. *(cf. Ex. 28:5-6)* The breastplate of judgment was the garment worn over the ephod, upon which the Urim and Thummin were attached. Presumably, this breastplate of judgment was so named because it represented the full, counsel and decisions of God's will for Israel. Essentially, as high priest, Aaron occupied the office of legislature whenever he entered the tabernacle on behalf of the people, for he bore each tribal name on this breastplate. In this capacity, Aaron, attended a sacred counsel meeting, in which he presented issues pertaining to divine precepts and societal influence. Through repentance, the saint does the same. When a saint comes to God in prayer on behalf of others, he presents the issues of his heart as they relate to himself and to others.

But what of the Urim and Thummin? Research of these provided no specificity about them. Therefore, both are nondescript substances. This lack of information seems to indicate that the Urim and Thummin were extraterrestrial in origin. They were not of this earth! Like the manna ("What is it?") which appeared briefly in the morning as a miracle food, *(cf. Ex. 16:14-36)* these two substances also seemed to be of heavenly origin and why not?

The tabernacle which Almighty God had revealed to Moses was also patterned after the original article located in heaven. So it is proper to consider the Urim and Thummin in this light as well.

The word *Urim* means, "light, the oracular brilliance, radiance, illumination, revelation, to see." The word *Thummin* means," perfections, completeness" (Strong's Exhaustive Concordance ref. #224 and 8558, pages 1099 and 1136) The spiritual application of the Urim and the Thummin are these. Each are types and shadows of Jesus Christ as well as the perfection of the saints. Specifically, the Urim represented the light of Jesus Christ, who is the Light of the world and as the Light of the glorious Gospel of Christ *(cf. John 1:7-9; 2 Cor. 4:46)* The Thummin, represented Jesus Christ as our perfected High Priest, after the order of Melchisedec. *(cf. Heb. 7:11-19)* Moreover, His perfection is to be found in the saints! *(cf. Eph. 4:11-15)*

The word *perfect* means, "truth, integrity, sincerely, undefiled, without spot or blemish, maturity, to be fully grown, mature." (Strong's Exhaustive Concordance, ref. # 8549, pages 814, 815) The fact that the Urim and Thummin were worn upon the breastplate of judgment suggests that Jesus Christ, as our Intercessor now, shall soon be revealed as the Judge of all the universe and the light of His judgment shall address man's carnality, which shall be conscripted with perfect and complete truth. *(cf. Rev. 20:4-15; Heb. 7:25; 12:23; Rom. 2:2; John 5:22, 30)*

Long Standing Disobedience

Israel's long standing disobedience to God's will and Word resulted in the scarceness of God's will and Word in the land. *(cf. 1 Sam. 3:1)* Eli, the blind Levitical priest and his two disobedient sons, Hophni and Phinehas, spoken of in 1 Samuel chapter 3, represent, for the saints of God, the blindness and disobedience of Israel's leadership and that of the churches of the New Testament. As a consequence, God removed the Thummin from the priestly garb as an indictment against a rebellious, stiff necked people, priests included. But why the Thummin? The Thummin was removed, because it meant perfection. That is too say, godly character was replaced with carnality. The people took the path of least restraint, as evidenced in their fervor for that residue of sin! The Urim however, was not removed, because it represented the absolute light of God. In spite of man's carnality though, Almighty God's immutability is absolute because He can not violate His own word which is established in heaven forever! No matter what mankind may do or say, God's word is secure, for without the Light of the world, mankind and God's created expanse would cease to exist. *(cf. Col. 1:15-19; Mal. 3:6; Heb. 13:8)*

According to Scripture, both substances were eventually lost. The last mention of either one is found in Nehemiah 7:65. **Truth #20: The revelation of a lifestyle of repentance is the light [knowledge] of salvation, for it qualifies faith!** *(cf. Col. 1:9-12; Jam. 2:14-26)* This lifestyle promotes godliness, not disobedience through carnal living. Through divine counsel and guidance, godliness is acquired, because the will of God is obeyed and His word is believed from the heart and known to the mind. **Truth #21: Since every saint is the temple [tabernacle] of the Holy Ghost, then each saint is also a priest of the Most High God and as a priest, must wear the spiritual articles of the Urim and the Thummin upon his heart, because what the breastplate of judgment was to the Old Testament priest, the breastplate of righteousness is to the New Testament saint!** He must minister to God in the light of revelation as a mature, living sacrifice and as a perfected saint exhibiting his knowledge of salvation, because no one can devote his life in repentance, unless he has received instruction in this doctrine! To this I add that true discipleship is consistent with progressive knowledge and holiness as unto the Lord, God and that alterations in traditional, theological theory and in practice must occur as are demanded by increasing light!

False Repentance

Truth #22: False repentance means to possess a deep regret for a decision to be set free, based solely on external circumstances. This impulsive behavior is often centered upon our self gratification and is not virtuous. Due to negative or hostile attitudes, a carnal person remains under the authority of an invisible task master. True repentance however, is virtuous and is not a pretense, since excuses are not made, due to unfavorable circumstances. Therefore, going back to Egypt or to that which is familiar is not an option.

Turning State's Evidence

A godly character places the saint in a position to be in authority over adverse circumstances in life. The saint of God must possess a zeal for repentance, because God possesses this same zeal to see His servants righteous and victorious in Him. This mind set is the result of an audacity of faith that says, "I am a mighty man of valor, in the service of the Most High God!" Moreover, repentance does not conceal evidence! Through a lifestyle of repentance, the saint of God turns state's evidence! God has a zeal to see a holy people. The saints of God must come into agreement with His passion, because there is power in agreement! *(cf. Amos 3:3)* There is no room for debate or circumvention of God's moral law, because repentance is not a platform to skirt issues of carnal living or to shirk from responsibility or to blame God, the devil or another.

Presumably, there are those in the worldly church who will make any excuse to justify their misery or bondage and avoid the challenge to change. Those who are insecure in their walk or ministry to which God has called them to, will dangle like a filthy rag, onto their tradition, their religion or their institutional indoctrinations as a comfort zone. True repentance, on the other hand, requires one to leave their milk bottle behind! Attitudinal injunctions and adjustments to these commands must be made in the church before a lifestyle of repentance may be conformed too!

The word of faith is the word of His righteousness and it does address man's carnality throughout Scripture. *(cf. Psa. 40:7)* The saints of God are therefore, instructed to renew the spirit of their minds and to pull down existing strongholds within their souls! But before these strongholds can be pulled down, an identification of these carnal fortresses must be made. Otherwise, these stockades shall remain in place for the brutish and the cattle-minded. To the carnally minded, their mentality is that they are just sinners saved by grace, nothing more and nothing less. How pathetic! Those embedded in their comfort zones resist change! So anyone who does not change, refuses or rejects repentance. They don't realize that this doctrine of God is for the Church, the knowledge of salvation and is for the saint, His instructions in righteousness! *(cf. John 7:16; 2 Tim. 3:15-17)*

We Must Repent of all Our Evils

Exodus 32:7-14

"And the Lord said unto Moses, Go, get thee down; for thy people which thou broughest out of the land of Egypt, **have corrupted themselves: They have turned** *aside quickly out of the way which I commanded them:* **they have made** *them a molten calf, and* **have worshiped** *it, and* **have sacrificed** *there unto,* **and said,** *These be thy gods, O Israel, which have brought thee up, out of the land of Egypt. And the Lord said, unto Moses, I have seen this people, and, behold, it is* **a stiff-necked people***: Now therefore let me alone, that my wrath may wax hot against them, and that I may consume them: and I will make of thee a great nation. And Moses besought the Lord his God, and said, Lord, why doth thy wrath wax hot against thy people, which thou has brought forth out of the land of Egypt*

*with thy great power, and with a mighty hand? Wherefore should the Egyptians speak, and say, For mischief did he bring them out, to slay them in the mountains, and to consume them from the face of the earth? Turn from thy fierce wrath, and repent of this evil against thy people. Remember Abraham, Isaac, and Israel, thy servants, to whom thou swarest by thine own self, and saidst unto them, I will multiply your seed as the stars of heaven, and all this land that I have spoken of will I give unto your seed, and they shall inherit it forever. And **the Lord repented** of the evil which he thought to do unto His people."* (emphasis mine)

Here in Exodus 32, we find the Hebrew people had corrupted themselves in the eyes of God, but in the absence of Moses, who was atop Mount Sinai receiving the *Ten Commandments*. Notice that Almighty God stated that the people had corrupted themselves. He did not state that the devil corrupted them, but they themselves. This observation then, forces the inquiry of just how much responsibility we must assume for our own actions, rather than simply too shrug it off as no big deal or to blame our conduct and behavior on God, the devil or another! **Truth #23: Repentance should be a demonstrated way of life, for it is the knowledge of salvation that targets the way of righteous-ness, which is the true path of life!**

Almighty God also said that they were a stiff-necked people! It seems that God became so angry that He lost His purpose of heart as to why He brought the people out of Egyptian bondage! Isn't it amazing to read that Moses, a created man, giving counsel to El Shaddai, Himself! It was as if the people were a hot potato tossed back and forth between God and Moses! In verse 12, Moses said, *"...turn from thy fierce wrath and repent of this evil against thy people."* The integrity of Moses was evident in his godly character! He was bold and such boldness was predicated by his audacious faith! This notability seeped into his life as repentance, so much so, that he counseled Almighty God to repent! Because Moses interceded on behalf of a stiff-necked people, God also repented of the evil which He intended against the people. Shouldn't the saints of God do the same? By embracing a lifestyle of repentance, in faith believing, the saints of God realize that life is not just about them individually, but more so about the salvation of souls. *(cf. Ezek. 9:4-6)*

Repentance is What We Must Do, Ahead of Time

Consider for a moment, an abusive, domestic relationship between a husband and wife. Due to the prolonged and tolerated carnality of both, the husband murders his wife. The wife would still be alive today, had he repented of his fierce rage against her ahead of time, no matter how justified he thought his rage to be. Here's a case in point involving a husband who actually did kill his wife, and whose identity and case number have been omitted. After crushing her skull with a framing hammer, he stuffed her body into a garage freezer, leaving it there on ice for three months. He then buried the body in a shallow two foot grave in a boy scout campground, only to be dug up by animals or unearthed by erosion. And it came to pass, that the skeletal remains were found, however no records existed to identify them. The forensic investigators hired a sculptor to make a plaster mold of the skull and to flesh it out with clay, revealing the facial image of the deceased. Once done, the sculpting was photographed and published. Soon, answers to the myriad of questions came pouring into the police. The deceased woman was identified, the manner of death was discovered and the husband was charged. Truly then, the dead do speak from their graves! *(cf. Gen. 4:8-10)* Although this crime is appalling in itself, it's ashen in the light of the more recent events of the Columbine High School shooting in Littleton, Colorado! I use these graphic examples to stress the point of the need for repentance, ahead of time, for our lives depend on it!

Let us not forget the mass murders and wholesale butchering of Iraqi citizens by their tyrannical leader, Saddam Hussein, either! With regards to the war with Iraq, although war may be necessary, what's really needed is repentance ahead of time, because the rage of a butcher and the self-righteousness of a nation shall never fulfill the righteousness of God. **Truth #24: Since God repented of this evil which He thought to do against the people for their rebellion, shouldn't we also repent of our evil thoughts and intentions against one another, ahead of time, before it's too late?** Eventually, God's fierce wrath shall lead to mankind's demise. Conversely, our wickedness condemns us to it! We all have evil thoughts, because of our carnality. Therefore, we must repent of these evil imaginations, ahead of time! Our evil thoughts are the iniquities (lie-based-thinking) often spoken of in Scripture. Anything that festers within the theater of the carnal mind is an iniquity, because it is a lie and therefore a premeditation and certainly a predominant thought. **Truth #25: Repentance therefore, is retaining a meditation on the things of God, and having a remorse for all our iniquitous premeditations!** *(cf. Psa. 119:11)*

Isaiah 26:21a
"For, behold, the Lord cometh out of His place to punish the inhabitants of the earth for their iniquity..."

The Reward of Iniquity or the Recompense of the Reward

Reward means, "a wage, hire, pay for service whether good or bad." Acts 1:18 speaks of the *"reward of iniquity."* Romans 6:23 states, *"that the wages of sin is death."* The Amplified Bible expresses it, *"For the wages which sin pays is death..."*

Psalm 91:8 AMP
"Only a spectator shall you be [yourself inaccessible in the se-

cret place of the Most High] as you witness the **reward** of the wicked." (emphasis mine)

Ruth 2:12
"The Lord recompense thy work, and a full reward be given thee of the Lord God of Israel, under whose wings thou art come to trust."

After all, even Judas Iscariot's iniquity lead to his suicide, as well as to his eternal demise just as our own iniquities often lead to wholesale murder and suicides as the newspapers do attest. In Hebrews 11:26 we read that Moses had *"respect unto the recompense of the reward."* Such respect pertains to the reward [compensation, recompense] of faith to the Word of God and obedience to the moral law of God. There is a song whose lyrics are, "He paid a debt, He did not owe; I owed a debt, I could not pay, I needed someone to wash my sins away..." Since Almighty God established His doctrine of repentance in the tabernacle construction and observances to it as the knowledge of salvation, in the process of time, the blood of Jesus Christ would also purchase that salvation and the provisions it affords. Therefore, it is now up to every person to come to faith in Jesus Christ, and for each saint to cultivate his own salvation through a lifestyle of repentance unto God! *(cf. Acts 20:21; Phil. 2:12)* In doing so, the saint demonstrates his respect for the reward.

The saints of God are purchased possessions and as such, they are The New Testament Church which belongs to God and not to the heathen, because of the purchased price paid. *(cf. 1 Cor. 6:20; 7:23)* As saints of God, we are to be living sacrifices unto Him. *(cf. Rom. 12:1)* A sacrifice that is not indebted to and spotted with the cravings of the flesh. A consecrated sacrifice that does not smoke, that does not consume intoxicants, that does not chew, that does not entertain or toy with smut or use profanity or any propensity that serves to gratify selfish indulgences. *(cf. Rom. 13:14)* We owe Almighty God our lives and because we do, we must show respect unto the reward. It's no different than the patriot who respects his nation's flag, because he is aware of the bloodshed behind it! Similarly, the saints of God must respect the flag of faith, for the very same reason!

The world may say, "I owe, I owe. Its off to work I go." or "Another day, another dollar!" But as saints of God, our creed should be that we are not debtors to the flesh! *(cf. Rom. 8:12)* **Truth #26: As any employee would receive a pay check for his work as compensation, it is therefore common knowledge then, that there does exist a wage, as a reward, for our carnality and a recompense for our respect to a lifestyle of repentance!**

Jeremiah 5:25
"Your iniquities have turned away these things, and your sins have with-holden good things from you."

Withdraw or Withdrawals

All physical addictions spawn objective symptoms of that which has been ingested and as any addict knows, there are withdrawals that his constitutional makeup shall endure. What the world may associate as an addiction or a craving, by design, the human body so poisoned, attempts to purge [withdraw] itself of the poisons placed into it. Where the former mind set implies that cravings of the body are in authority over the addict, the latter and most appropriate mind set, declares that the body is in authority over the craving! It's a matter of understanding the indigenous position all people possess by design, because we were created for the good and not for the bad.

The Untouchables

Psalm 91:8
"Only a spectator shall you be [yourself inaccessible in the secret place of the Most High] as you witness the reward of the wicked."

When the saint of God abides behind the veil, in that secret place [Holy of Holies, shrine, closet], he is in the very presence of God! Here, the saint remains untouchable, for he has touched and has been touched. A lifestyle of repentance therefore, touches God! Similarly, everybody has a soft spot. You know, that certain place of the body or soul, which is more sensitive than other areas. Well, Almighty God has a soft spot as well. It's His heart! **Truth #27: Through a lifestyle of repentance, the saint touches God's soft spot!** Why? Because tenderness denotes intimacy and the saint experiences both in the secret place of the Most High! Therefore, the saints of God remain untouchable so long as they touch the soft spot of God. Conversely, a soft spot also means to be easily injured or offended. Such hearts are protected, not with maturity or genuine love, but with manipulative tactics of abuse, arrogance, control and domination. Explosive emotional outbursts and random acts of violence seem to be the carnal tendencies of such a heart as this. All this, just to protect the one whose heart is fragile, but always at the expense of the hearts and lives of others!

Notes:

Chapter 4
Repentance in the Book of Leviticus

Carnal Knowledge is the Knowledge of Salvation

The theme of this book is, How can sinful man approach a Holy God? It's key words are *Access* and *Holiness* and its first seven chapters address the ceremonial laws pertaining to the specific offerings which Almighty God mandated the Hebrews to obey. Each instituted offering (oblation), was to be obeyed with strict attention to detail by both the priest and the individual. This protocol was to be kept, but before they could be observed, the people first had to be taught. This knowledge forced personal accountability for without this knowledge, God's laws could not be obeyed by Moses, Aaron or anyone. Therefore, God saw to it that man's carnal ignorance was to be replaced with specific carnal knowledge, which is the knowledge of one's carnality, ergo, the knowledge of salvation. However, for ages past, the mind set has been, "Ignorance is bliss." and "What we don't know, won't hurt us." Carnal knowledge is never acquired by responding to an evangelistic or otherwise orchestrated altar call alone, although this could be a start. Salvation must involve specific knowledge and wisdom, after conversion. Otherwise, the new convert remains in his carnal ignorance. Hence, carnal knowledge, as it relates to repentance, is unquestionably the knowledge of salvation! True discipleship therefore, involves instruction in righteousness, and not the indoctrination of some denominational dogma.

Sometime ago, in the preparation for this investigation, I had asked certain lay people of several Roman Catholic Churches if they could define for me "carnal knowledge." To the man or woman, not a single lay person could give me an answer. I finally, did ask a priest and his reply was, "The spirit is willing but the flesh is weak." *(cf. Matt. 26:41)* It is important to realize that ignorance abounds within the traditional church. So many of our little catch phrases and words are just empty containers to the individual, without meaning or purpose. They are often uttered as nebulous fillers, lacking content and quality. If asked of its meaning, oftentimes the person making such remarks such as, "yada, yada, yada" has no idea as to why or what they said!

In the eyes of God, dear saint, we all have an obligation to know, because specific knowledge of God's moral law, qualifies what is said or believed. Come to think of it, the root word of ignorance is ignore. Just because something is ignored, does not necessarily mean that "it" will fade away. Whereas an ostrich may stick its head in the sand, it seems that most Christians have stuck their heads in the clouds of ignorance! As far as God is concerned, when His moral law is ignored, His commandments are also disregarded, neglected and disobeyed! Consequently, what we don't know can actually hurt us. Ignorance is not bliss! So as you can see, our very lives depend on specific carnal knowledge!

Isaiah 33:6
"And wisdom and knowledge shall be the stability of thy times, and [the] strength of thy salvation: the fear of the Lord is his treasure. (cf. Hos. 4:6; Prov. 1:7) (brackets mine)

1 Timothy 1:6-7 AMP
"But certain individuals have missed the mark on this very matter [and] have wandered away into vain arguments and dis-

cussions and purposeless talk. They are ambitious to be doctors of the Law (teachers of the Mosaic ritual), but they have no understanding either of the words and terms they use or of the subjects about which they make [such] dogmatic assertions."

Leviticus 5:18
"...and the priest shall make an atonement for him concerning his ignorance wherein he erred and wist it not, and it shall be forgiven him."

The Hebrew translation for the word *wist* is "yada." As used in this verse it means, "to show or possess no regard or diligence for God's Word. It means to bend the rules." (Strong's Exhaustive Concordance Heb. ref. #3045, page 47) Colloquially, it means to circumvent the law, or to get away with something. It's the attitude that it's no big deal! *(cf. Jer. 3:9)* Couple this with the sin of ignorance and ungodly habits and it should be evident that such people are spiritually depraved and morally deprived! These have no concept of spiritual matters apart from of the goose bump, make me feel good, *charismaniac* message or movement. The result being, their ignorance of their old carnal nature remains as an unknown nature, at that! Why? Because the emphasis is placed upon grace, in the form of blessings only and not repentance! This is very evident, because the proof is found in the theme of the message or movement, itself. The first syllable of the word, *charismatic*, is charis. *Charis* is the Greek word for grace! (Vine's Expository Dictionary, page 169) Try as one may to address the one-dimensional ignorance of their carnality or to correct a particular character flaw and the response would be defiance, because people just don't want to be told what to do or to be told that they have done wrong! The most common remark would be, "Just who do you think you are?" or "Who made you judge and jury?"

Leviticus 4:1-4

*"And the Lord spake unto Moses, saying, Speak unto the children of Israel, saying, If a soul shall sin through ignorance against any of the commandments of the Lord **concerning things which ought not to be done**, and shall do against any of them: If the priest that is anointed do sin according to the sin of the people; then let him bring for his sin, which he hath sinned, a young bullock without blemish unto the Lord for a sin offering. And he shall bring the bullock unto the door of the tabernacle of the congregation before the Lord; and shall lay his hand upon the bullock's head, and kill the bullock before the Lord."* (emphasis mine)

These passages teach that there is a sin of ignorance. The remainder of the chapter tells of the specific requirements to remedy this sin within the soul of the individual, a priest, of a ruler or of the congregation. Knowing that not all Hebrew citizens were necessarily affluent, Almighty God made provision for all class structures and especially for the priests, for He is no respecter of persons. The sin of ignorance was any sin of a physical or sensual sort and applied to carnality. Such ignorance is still very much prevalent within the soul of man today, no matter how suave he may be or thinks he is. Our unknown carnal nature applies to our old nature. Our old nature consists of bantering theories, concepts, opinions, reasoning, imaginations, ideologies, surmising, beliefs, bad or wrong attitudes, patterns of traditional thinking or speaking which are evident in one's behavior and conduct. These are observed publicly through one's character, for we are known by such. All these and so much more, are the works of an unregenerate, uncapitulated nature of carnality, and these are all objective symptoms of the strongholds within the soul of the individual.

As long as humanity remains on this earth, man's carnality shall exist within his soul and it must be contended with! *(cf. Isa. 22:14)* Therefore, it is vital that God's multi-dimensional Word be applied to the depths of our carnality. Unfortunately, most people camp out on just the surface level, when Almighty God desires that His truths sink deep into the darkened depths of man's soul, where the strongholds of his carnality are rooted. Afflictions and the torments of a man are found in his soul and his carnality is the culprit. Man's carnality provides the nutrients and the iniquity within the unregenerate soul of man is the seed bed for all that his carnality produces! **Truth #28: Through a lifestyle of repentance, the soul is afflicted even to the very depths of one's carnality!**

The Head of the Bull is Cattle Mindedness

Brutish is an Old Testament word which means "stupid, foolishness, cattle minded, cattle mindedness, herd mentality." (Strong's Exhaustive Concordance Heb. ref. #1197, 1198, page 43) The priest was required to lay his hand on the head of the bullock to be sacrificed. The bull's head represented the individual and more specifically, the spirit of his mind. As long as a man is in his carnality, God considers him to be brutish because, his carnality unequivocally connotes cattle mindedness! It is evident, therefore, that the majority of congregations are nothing more than stockyards, wherein reside herds of bovine with the head of the bull being their spiritual leader or their denominational dogma! This explanation conveys the meaning of bullheadedness, doesn't it? It is here, where sacred cows are corralled and then slaughtered on the slab of innocuous preaching! Where's the beef? Everybody moo!

By laying his hand on the bull's head, the priest, in the presence of the sinner, would then plead the blood of atonement over the individual who presented the offering. This offering had to cost the sinner something! It had to be his and not that of another. **Truth #29: Through a lifestyle of repentance, the sacred cows of carnality are slaughtered as sin offerings of atonement for our ignorance!**

It has been commonly accepted that as the priest placed his hand upon the head of the animal to be sacrificed, a sin transfer occurred between the individual sinner and the animal. Although this is a spiritual operation, there is another which seemingly has been overlooked. It's the spiritual truth of binding, which involved a vow and the commitment to keep it whenever the priest placed his hand on the head of the bull. A spiritual submission did occur, because he bound the spirit of the mind of the sinner to the Mind of the Spirit of God! The intent being that integrity, as a virtue of godliness, would be pursued by the penitent, voluntarily yielding his intellect, intuitions, reasoning and will, all of which are faculties of his mind, to God. *(cf. Num. 30:2; 1 Kgs. 9:4-5; 1 Cor. 2:16)*

Job 27:5
"*God forbid that I should justify you: till I die I will not remove mine integrity from me.*"

Proverbs 10:6-7
"*Blessings are upon the **head** of the just: but violence covereth the mouth of the wicked. The **memory** of the just is blessed: but the name of the wicked shall rot.*" (emphasis mine)

Romans 8:27
"*And he that searcheth the hearts knoweth what is the mind of the Spirit, because He maketh intercession for the saints according to the will of God.*"

Philippians 2:5
"*Let this mind be in you which was also in Christ, Jesus:*"

A Law Abiding Citizen

Truly, to be a law abiding citizen requires one to possess, at least a familiarity to certain laws. However, there are those who possess particular working knowledge of the laws of science and of the land as they relate to specifics. An attorney for example, has a law practice of jurisprudence, because he possesses specific working knowledge of the law. A physician has a medical practice, because the doctor possesses specific working knowledge of the laws pertaining to medical science. A law enforcement officer also has specific working knowledge of the Penal Code, Vehicle Code and other related codes pertaining to the citizenry and crime. Again, any CEO would likewise possess working knowledge of the tax laws, as a means to protect his investments and corporate profits and expenditures through his specific knowledge of tax shelters and loopholes in the tax laws. Finally, a military man would also possess specific knowledge and stratagems, pertaining to warfare in the defense of freedom. Likewise, God desires that His saints, also possess specific working knowledge pertaining to His moral laws which when obeyed, employ the law of faith and the law of repentance. Otherwise, ignorance remains, by choice of the individual, in that he chooses to squander his gifts and callings, due to a superficial rendering of biblical truth.

Although Almighty God knows how tragic experiences have shocked the psyche of His people and how these have impacted the function of a person's character, He will not condone their doggedness to hold on to these dysfunctions! The saint of God must realize that God's Word is the remedy for man's carnal tragedy! **Truth #30: Through specific, working knowledge of the law of faith and repentance, the saint exercises his legal right as a law abiding citizen of heaven!**

Repentance is the Affliction of the Soul

Leviticus 16:30-31
*"For on that day shall the priest make an atonement for you, to cleanse you, **that** ye may be clean from all your sins before the*

Lord. It shall be a Sabbath of rest unto you, and **ye shall afflict your souls**, *by a statute forever."* (emphasis mine)

The word *afflict* as used here means, "to cause distress, to provoke, to agitate, to mortify, to submit self, to chasten self." (Strong's Exhaustive Concordance Heb, ref.# 6031, page 90) **Truth #31: Just as the bull was killed at the altar of sacrifice, similarly, repentance, for the saints of God, involves a killing! It requires the saints of God to die to the impulses of self gratification and to mortify their carnality, because the cross that most carry, is not the cross that they must carry!** *(cf. Lev. 23:26-32; Mk. 8:34-38)*

Romans 8:13 AMP
"For if you live according to [the dictates of] the flesh, you will surely die. But if through the power of the [Holy] Spirit you are [habitually] putting to death (making extinct, deadening) the [evil] deeds prompted by the body, you shall [really and genuinely] live forever."

The Law of Leprosy

In Leviticus 13, we read of the laws and tokens in the detection of the disease called leprosy. Leprosy had then, as it does now, objective symptoms which signified to the masses that a contagious bacteria did exist. In Leviticus 14, we read of the cleansing remedy of the leper and the symptoms of leprosy within a leprous house. Both chapters showed when a physical affliction to the skin was leprous or not or when the interior walls of a house were, in fact contaminated (unclean or clean). The law of leprosy therefore stipulated that if a condition of leprosy did exist, then the individual and his house, so infected, were said to be unclean until proven otherwise.

Leprous America

In the spring of 1981, America and the world, were introduced to a very contagious disease called *AIDS*. Immediately, upon learning of this, the witness of my heart was leprosy because, like AIDS, it is incurable, although its symptoms can be suppressed. Only a miracle of God can cure leprosy, and so it is with Aids. *(cf. Lk. 17:11-19)* More recently, when in the aftermath of the 9-11-01 attacks on America, the Center for Disease Control (CDC) personnel responded to the several state localities where anthrax spores were detected. Americans watched the CDC personnel, in their full body hazmat suits, enter and then exit the government buildings where these spores were found. What was so amazing was the great lengths taken to contain these spores, neutralize them and then remove all contaminated materials. These men exited the buildings with full, large, black, plastic trash bags in hand as they breathed through their respirators. What a cumbersome task it was. All this gallant attention to detail was brought about by these apparent bio-attacks upon Americans and our installations. These historic events are comparable to the scriptural context of Leviticus chapters 13 and especially to 14. **Truth #32: What the law of leprosy was to the disease, the law of repentance is to the residue of sin, our carnality; and what was symptomatic of leprosy to the people then, is indicative of the sin spores of carnality for people today!**

Weapons of Mass Destruction

Just as the CDC personnel were careful to suppress the potential outbreak of anthrax, and just as these men were careful to investigate and eradicate these anthrax spores from our government buildings, likewise is God careful not to permit sin spores to enter into His house and neither should we! God is telling America there are sin spores resident within her soul! It's called carnality! And just as these anthrax spores were mailed, God is also telling the traditional church that we are all carriers and are therefore contaminated! Truly, our Omniscient God has literally read our mail!

These sin spores are also symptomatic of other known attributes of sin such as psychosomatic illnesses, sexually transmitted diseases, blood diseases, abortion issues, murders, suicide, all manner of crime, etc. Yes, America is defiled, because her soul is unclean! Man's carnality is a weapon of mass destruction for wickedness is man's own device! Literally, thousands die each day as a result of these sin spores and throughout history, millions more have already perished unaware of the effects of their own carnality!

A Day to Atone and a Day of Salvation

Everybody knows that the word *day* means or refers to a 24 hour period of time. It also refers to an era or an age in history such as the day of discovery, the Jurassic age or the day of salvation. However, as far as western civilization is concerned, our misunderstanding and lack of scriptural intent seems to be more refined, so much so, that the depths of spiritual insight has been, for the most part, processed from the meal of God's Word, due to the excessive milling process of denominationalism. This is evident when you consider repentance, as the doctrine of God and as the knowledge of salvation! Just the mere mention of repentance, causes most people to become indifferent, even indignant! Again, it is for this purpose that this investigative work is offered.

Leviticus 23:27-29

*"Also on the tenth **day** of this seventh month **there shall** be a day of atonement: it shall be a holy convocation unto you; and **ye shall afflict your souls**, and offer an offering made by fire unto the Lord. And ye shall do no work in that same day: for it is a day of atone-*

ment, to make an atonement for you before the Lord your God. For **whatsoever soul it be that shall not be afflicted** in that same day, shall be cut off from among his people." (emphasis mine)

2 Corinthians 6:2
"(For he saith, I have heard thee in a time accepted, and in the day of salvation have I succoured thee: behold, now is the accepted time, now is the day of salvation.)"

I've heard it said from some pulpits that the word *atonement*, when broken down into syllables (at-one-ment), is a simple way to understand its meaning. This deplorable assessment is like the elevator that won't go all the way to the top! This grammar lesson has never done anything to enhance the saint's understanding of the spiritual empowerment of God's grace, nor the significance of this foundational truth of The Gospel message. How tragic that spiritual insight has plummeted so short of this truth of salvation. This ignorance, in the rank and file of leadership, is the embryo of those who doubt or disbelieve that Jesus Christ died for the sins of the world and that there are, in their estimation, others paths to eternal life! No wonder the people of this land are so confused and befuddled about religion and their relationship with God through Christ!

John 14:6
"Jesus saith unto him, I am the way, the truth and the life; No man cometh unto the Father but by me."

Acts 4:12
"Neither is there salvation in any other: for there is none other name under heaven given among men, whereby we **must** *be saved."(cf. John 3:3-7, 6:47-58)* (emphasis mine)

According to the Vine's Expositor Dictionary on page 86, the word, *atonement* is foreign to the Greek Bible, with respect to God whether in the Septuagint or the New Testament translations. But this does not invalidate atonement, for it is strictly a ceremonial Old Testament application. From this viewpoint then, *atonement* means "to plead the blood repeatedly, for the remission of sins." Why? Because a blood sacrifice was offered repeatedly for the remission of sins. However, in the New Testament, such synonymous words as propitiation, reconciliation and mercy seat are used to represent this spiritual import through the atoning work of Jesus Christ, once and for all. Moreover, for the saint of God, personal atonement also applies to a lifestyle of repentance, in the day of his living, for this atonement is the vow of the saint's integrity as his corresponding action to the atonement found in the blood of Christ! *(cf. Rom. 3:25, 5:11; 2 Cor. 5:18-19; Heb. 9:5; 1 John 2:2, 4:10)* Even 2 Corinthians 6:2 declares, there is a day of salvation as an *"accepted time."* The Amplified Bible translates it as the *"time of favor."* Either way, Paul the Apostle spoke of a propitiation for his day as well as ours.

To Appease the Gods

The Apostle Paul used the word *propitiation* in his letter to the Romans in chapter 3 verse 25. His intent was to communicate to these people, whose practice was to appease their false gods, the truth of atonement which Almighty God had already established and provided through Jesus Christ. Paul wanted to instruct these idolaters that God the Father, had already dealt with sin so that He could show mercy to the people, specifically, to the sinner soon to be converted in the removal of his guilt and for the remission of his sins. Paul wanted to convey to the Romans this spiritual truth of atonement that by God's own act, He alone, provided deliverance from justly deserved wrath and through faith in the blood of Christ, all who enter in become heirs and participants with God the Father's covenant of grace.

Religion is fear based and it incarcerates its agents. Never is God to be reconciled to man in and through a work ethic of wood, hay or stubble, because this entrenched psychology is the seed bed of false religions. Rather, God has reconciled the world to Himself, by Himself. *(cf. 2 Cor. 5:18-19)* Where *reconcile* pertains to our spiritual rebirth, *reconciliation* (atonement) pertains to the regeneration of our soul, wherein lies carnality as that residue of sin. *(cf. 2 Cor. 5:17-21)*

Fodder for the Gods

It's been said that sharks are unpredictable. Whether they are or not is not the issue here, but as to appeasing false gods, presumably, these idolaters did believe that their false deities were unpredictable, even moody; and to the Roman, a false god was either a man or a statue. Therefore, these deities had to be pacified for fear of retribution. Consider the practice of the blood sacrifices of now extinct civilizations and that of the Old Testament people, especially the children who were fodder for the gods. Just imagine yourself as a parent who, knowing that one day, a cleric would appear at your home demanding your child as fuel for the furnace of Molech, not to mention the stark raving terror your son or daughter would have felt! Presently, while America is at war with the Iraqi regime of Saddam Hussein, children are kidnaped from their homes at gun point by Saddam's henchmen to discourage the child's family and society, as a whole, from resisting his rule by revolution. The terror these children experience as fodder for the god known as Saddam Hussein, only compares to the historical accounts which the Bible, itself addresses. *(cf. Lev. 18:21; Jer. 32:35)*

Such occult practices were fear based and motivated by ignorance of the knowledge of salvation! As it was then, so it remains today, that people perish for lack of specific, working knowledge. Because knowledge is rejected, in its place religious observances have become the predominate rule. It was for this reason also that Paul spoke of the *"Gospel rule"* to the saints in Galatia.

Galatians 6:16 AMP
"Peace and mercy be upon all who walk by this rule [who discipline themselves and regulate their lives by this principle], even upon the [true] Israel of God!"

Psalm 125:5 AMP
"As for such as turn aside to their crooked ways [of indifference to God], the Lord will lead them forth with the workers of iniquity. Peace be upon Israel!"

The Law of Repentance

Leviticus 23:27-29 speaks of the day of atonement wherein no man was to work and that he was to afflict his soul. Just as Aaron, the high priest, was to continually come before the Lord, God wearing the breastplate of judgment and the Urim and the Thummin, so too were the Hebrews to afflict their souls for themselves, which Aaron also did on their behalf. The affliction of their soul was a demonstration of the application of the spiritual truth of the reconciliation of their soul back to God! In Isaiah 53, we read of the sufferings of Christ. In light of appeasement, such affliction and oppression which Jesus endured, pleased [satisfied as a bond] the Father in an accepted or favorable time to make His soul an offering for man's sin. *(cf. Isa. 53:2-12)* Since Calvary, Jesus Christ, as High Priest, is presently making intercession for His saints. *(cf. Heb. 7:25)* Aaron did the same as Moses. Therefore, this law of repentance was too be obeyed by doing and not just then, but by every saint of God today! However, the priesthood has since changed and of necessity the law must also change, from the ceremonial law of the Old Testament sacrifices, to the law of the Spirit of life in the New Testament. But the application is still the same, that being the atonement of the soul! *(cf. Heb. 7:11-13; Rom. 8:2)*

Whereas, human sacrifices were fodder for the gods, Jesus Christ, who was born to die, became the sacrificial Lamb of the one, true God so that man would no longer be deceived by occultism. The one, true God was so pleased through the death of His Son, Jesus Christ that the soul of Jesus was the offering for the sin within the soul of man! It's a classic case of an eye for an eye and a tooth for a tooth. **Truth #33: The reign of the inward work of God's righteousness upon the heart and soul of man is the effect of the law of repentance, because the reconciliation of his soul, as a living sacrifice, is the saint's reasonable service!** *(cf. Rom. 12:1)*

To Please Almighty God

The executioner may say to the condemned, "Make your peace and prepare to meet your maker." Others may also say, "I made my peace with the man upstairs." But unless Jesus Christ is allowed to enter into one's heart, through faith in His atoning blood, there is no peace with God! The Word of God tells us clearly that only Jesus Christ is our Peace Who breaks down the wall that separates us from Almighty God. *(cf. Eph. 2:14)* It is only then that God is pleased. *(cf. Heb. 10:38, 11:6; 1 Thes. 2:4, 4:1; Psa.116:15; Prov. 16:7)* **Truth #34: Throughout life, the saint of God separates himself from all worldly distractions, either sensory or psychologically, composing himself with the quiet preparations of his heart, because he knows that he must employ serious calculations of meekness to please his God!** The saint's meekness is not to be mistaken as weakness, but of strength, for the joy of the Lord is his strength for battle! The saint of God is keenly aware of the pollution within his soul. He knows that his carnality is most detestable in the eyes of God and that a battle waged against his carnality is necessary to suppress its influence upon his character/heart.

Our Atonement is Our Involvement

An imbalance exists within the churches of the New Testament with regards to the atoning blood of Christ and the saint's walk of faith as a corresponding action to it. We say that we agree that Jesus did shed His precious blood for the remission of our sins and yet we fail to see that our atonement is also our involvement! Jesus Christ paved the way at Calvary, but the saints of God must still travel down this road, called repentance! Heretofore, for the church, repentance has long since become a road less traveled! *(cf. 2 Pet. 3:9; Mat. 7:13-14)*

Although Jesus Christ is our Savior, it is up to the individual to possess his vessel and then to cultivate this salvation provided. **Truth #35: The saint's involvement is the atonement of his soul, because a lifestyle of repentance is the road less traveled! Therefore, the knowledge of the atoning work of Jesus Christ is the knowledge of salvation and repentance is that pathway of instruction in the way of righteousness!**

Isaiah 33:6
"And wisdom and knowledge shall be the stability of thy times, and [the] strength of [thy] salvation: the fear of the Lord is his treasure." (cf. 2 Tim. 3:15-16; John 10:9, 11:25, 14:6; Lk. 19:9; Acts 4:12, 5:31; Psa. 118:14, 21) (brackets mine)

1 Timothy 4:7-8, 16
"But refuse profane and old wives fables, and exercise thyself rather unto godliness. For bodily exercise profiteth little: but godliness is profitable unto all things, having promise of the life that now is, and of that which is to come. Take heed unto thyself, and unto the doctrine; continue in them: for in doing this thou shalt

both save thyself, and them that hear thee."

The House of Replies

According to the Vine's Expository Dictionary, pages 37-39, the word *afflict* as used in Leviticus chapter 23 means, "anguish, burdened, distress, persecution, tribulation, trouble." (not all inclusive) It implies that afflict is primarily a New Testament word. The Strong's Exhaustive Concordance, (Heb. ref. # 1042, page 20; 6030, page 90) also defines *afflict* to mean, "to depress, brow beat, abase self, chasten self, humble self, submit self, pay attention to, to respond, give account of or to, to give answer to, house of replies."

Keeping atonement in mind, to afflict one's soul then, is a self-examination and introspection as a personal obligation. A personal accountability must be acquired. But in this day of promiscuity and self gratification, such obligations to answer to the moral laws of God for one's conduct and behavior has been sullied as being out of vogue. No longer is it stylish to retain one's integrity, and honor or to remain upright!

In court, however, the judge will ask the offender charged, "How do you plea?" Or "What is your plea to these charges?" In so stating, the judge forces the issue of accountability in the courtroom, for it is, for the criminal, his first House of Replies! When the offender is sentenced to imprisonment, fined or given the death sentence, he shall, one way or the other, answer for his crime!

The correctional facility too, is a house of replies in that the inmate answers for the charges by doing time. As already mentioned, the jail cell was originally known as the cell of penitence. It was here, in his assigned house of reply that the inmate was to reconcile his ways back to God and to society. To be a true prisoner of Jesus Christ, therefore requires every saint to go to his cell of penitence daily, as his house of reply, just as the inmate who lives out the duration of his sentence behind bars. In this, a lifestyle of repentance is developed and the saint becomes wise unto salvation. **Truth #36: Just as the judge forces the issue of accountability to the offender, a lifestyle of repentance also forces the issue of carnality to the saint for without repentance, he remains a fugitive!** *(cf. Isa. 26:9)*

A Cell Within a Box

Just as an onion consists of layers, and just as there may be smaller boxes within a larger box, and just as the wilderness tabernacle consisted of three courts within a larger, periphery court, so too then are there [jail] cells within pods. Whereas, the outer court was a public display, the inner court was secluded with the Holy of Holies being most restricted. *(cf. Ex. 35-40)* Similarly, there are boundaries in one's life. As shown, from the courtroom to the prison to the jail cell, each represents a house of reply, but at varying levels of subjectivity. Where the courtroom is more of a public humiliation, the jail cell is the most private introspection. **Truth #37: A lifestyle of repentance is most subjective, for it is the private examination and introspection of self as a cell within a box!**

As another illustration, consider a jewelry box. By comparison to other boxes, the jewelry box is quite small. Yet, in spite of its size, the contents are always more extravagant. Even the box itself has a distinct appearance compared to other generic boxes. Surely the jewelry, though it is small and very costly, is cherished above most other material possessions. The fact that jewelry is worn to compliment the complexion and to some degree enhance the individual's countenance, confirms the great prestige given to the precious stone. The point being, the smaller the box, the greater the treasure. That which is the least has greater significance and value. **Truth #38: Whereas, the brilliance of a diamond's fire is seen in its depth and cut, so too** is the brilliance of a lifestyle of repentance seen in the depth and cut of the saint's heart and soul, for he has become God's precious stone and in so doing, he is valuable!

Malachi 3:17
"And they shall be mine, saith the Lord of Hosts, in that day when I make up my jewels; and I will spare them, as a man spareth his own son that serveth him. (cf. Prov. 1:2-9; Isa. 28:16)

Matthew 18:3-4
"And said, Verily I say unto you, Except ye be converted, and become as little children, ye shall not enter into the kingdom of heaven. Whosoever therefore shall humble himself as this little child, the same is the greatest in the kingdom of heaven." (cf. Matt. 5:19, 23:11)

Zechariah 9:16
"And the Lord their God shall save them in that day as the flock of his people: for they shall be as the stones of a crown, lifted up as an ensign upon his land."

1 John 4:4
"Ye are of God, little children, and have overcome them, because greater is he that is in you than he that is in the world."

Notes:

Chapter 5
Repentance in the Book of Numbers

To Bear the Iniquity

In chapters 16 and 17, Scripture relates of a conspiracy and its ensuing rebellion which existed within the ranks of the Levitical priesthood. Specifically, in chapter 16, Korah, a levitical priest, conspired against God and Moses. He marshaled two hundred fifty other levitical priests to stand with him and against Moses. Eventually, Almighty God had the last word. He charged that hell enlarge herself and open wide her mouth. So the earth opened wide and swallowed all the conspirators, putting a close to this rebellion. *(cf. Num. 16:1-34)*

Isaiah 5:13,14
"Therefore my people are gone into captivity, because they have no knowledge: and their honorable men are famished, and their multitude dried up with thirst. Therefore hell hath enlarged herself, and opened her mouth without measure: and their glory, and their multitude, and their pomp, and he that rejoiceth, shall descend into it."

The Smoking Gun/Relic

Numbers 16:38
"The censers of these sinners against their own souls, let them make broad plates for a covering of the altar: for they offered them before the Lord, therefore, they are hallowed: and they shall be a

sign unto the children of Israel."

This verse states in part, *"...the censers of these sinners against their own souls..."* This verse teaches that man's carnality is a smoking gun/relic and is therefore lethal to a man's heart, because carnality resides within his soul! Almighty God commanded Moses to take the two hundred fifty censers, which each of the two hundred fifty priests had, and fashion them into broad plates for a covering, and to affix the plates to the altar, for a memorial of this insurgency. Not only were these tangible plates a physical memorial, but Almighty God recorded this rebellion in a register, which I call the "Book of Rebellion" *(cf. Isa. 30:8-9)* as its contains all the sins of the wicked. *(cf. Rev. 20:11-15)* So as you can see, God once again, validates that repentance memorializes man's carnality and a book of rebellion records the crimes of perpetrators!

Then in verse 41, Scripture conveys that the Israelites also murmured against Moses and Aaron on the following day! In essence, they stated to both, You killed the people of God! You murdered our spiritual leaders! The remainder of chapter 16 suggests that Almighty God wanted to destroy the entire assembly of the nefarious, *(cf. 16:20-22)* but through the atonement and repentance of Moses and Aaron, *(vs. 22)* such total destruction was averted. All this to show that man's iniquity is part and parcel to his carnality. **Truth #39: To bear the iniquity, means to be aware of the smoking gun/relic that is one's carnality and to consider its lethal effects upon the heart and soul!**

Numbers 18:1
"And the Lord said unto Aaron, Thou and thy sons and thy father's house with thee shall bear the iniquity of the sanctuary: and thou and thy sons with thee shall bear the iniquity of your priesthood."

Being a servant/minister is deeper and greater than merely doing a job for God. A lifestyle of repentance is a life long career, for it's the saint's profession of faith. In chapter 18, God held the priesthood liable and to account in the performance of their temple service, because leadership demands a heavier accountability! Not only did God hold them as answerable to their duty, but also to their calling! In other words, the priests were to know that their calling corresponded to their duty and that a spirit of excellency was expected!

The iniquity spoken of in the verse above, denotes the iniquity of the priesthood found in chapters 16 and 17. The murmuring of the people was a gripe, a grumble and a complaint against the leadership of Moses and Aaron! Their carping was also a unified voice of usurpation on behalf of the wrong leadership.

Leadership as a Barometer

Today iniquity has deepened within the sacred halls of leadership. When leading sports figures are indoctrinated into the sports hall of fame in spite of their demonstrated carnality [character flaws], or when government officials can remain in office regardless of their promiscuities and their "pork barrel" tactics involving theft or greed for their own personal gain, truth has fallen in the streets! *(cf. Isa. 59:2-15)* When corporate leadership falls prey to greed and when spiritual leadership falls victim to its own promiscuity, possessions and presumptions, God's truth has fallen to the gutter and vomit covers the table of spiritual and corporate management! *(cf. Isa. 28:7-8; 1 Cor. 10:21)* Almighty God's standard of righteousness demands that leadership positions be occupied by statesmen and not politicians, whose convictions are that of a servant of the people and not of despot over the people! Where a *statesman* is selfless and therefore virtuous, a *politician* is a self promoting ingratiate and a gratuitous thief! Spiritual leadership is a spiritual barometer, because it too is a cross section of society. It is a by-product of it and as the church goes, so goes the nation, because domestic and civil foundations have been eroded.

Spiritual leadership refers to the governing offices within the church. They are apostle, prophet, evangelist, pastor, teacher *(cf. Eph. 4:11-13)* and as such, they are gifts to the Body of Christ. But too many leaders have allowed their integrity to become compromised and their pulpit responsibilities to become gutter trash! Because truth has fallen, there remains little evidence of justice, mercy, kindness and humility and in its place resides incredulous pride. *(cf. Isa. 14:13-14; Mi. 6:8; Matt. 23:23)* On the other hand, through a lifestyle of repentance, integrity and honor are esteemed, for as God stated to Israel, *"Ye shall not lack a man [leader] to be ruler in Israel." (cf. 2 Chron. 7:18; Isa. 3:1-15; Phil. 4:1-9)* To keep the charge then, is to keep the office!

Keep the Charge

Any charge expressed denotes the character and intent of the one giving it. And with every charge, there is an obligation and an expectancy of performance or function. **Truth #40: Whereas, a charge improves morale, repentance as a personal charge, enhances one's salvation!** Where there is no charge, the saint becomes passive, shiftless, aimless and complacent! **Truth #41: A lifestyle of repentance displaces complacency much like an object would displace water with its mass or volume, because the weight of a lifestyle of repentance pierces the depths of one's carnality!** The water still exists all around, but the weight of it pierces the depths. So it is with carnality. As long as mankind inhabits this earth, carnality shall also exist within the darkened depths of his soul.

2 Timothy 4:1-3
"I charge thee therefore before God, and the Lord Jesus Christ,

who shall judge the quick and the dead at his appearing and his kingdom; Preach the word, be instant in season, out of season; reprove, rebuke, exhort with all longsuffering and doctrine. For the time will come when they will not endure sound doctrine..."

Paul charged young Timothy to preach God's Word with force and urgency, because the iniquities and unrighteousness of the inhabitants of the earth shall soon be judged! *(cf. Isa. 26:9-10, 21; Rev. 20:11-15)* Paul said this some 2000 years ago. How prevalent then, is this charge for the church today?

Proverbs 16:17
"The highway of the upright is to depart from evil: he that keepeth his way shall preserve his soul."

Proverbs 19:16
"He that keepeth the commandments keepeth his own soul; but he that despiseth his ways shall die."

1 Peter 4:17-18
"For the time is come that judgment begin at the house of God; and if it first begin at us, what shall the end of them that obey not the gospel of God? And if the righteous scarcely be saved, where shall the ungodly and the sinner appear?"

Hebrews 3:6
"But Christ as a son over his own house; whose house are we, if we hold fast the confidence and the rejoicing of the hope firm unto the end."

A Now Word of Faith is not to be Repented of

Numbers 23:19-20
"God is not a man, that he should lie; neither the son of man,

that he should repent: hath he said, and shall he not do it? Or hath he spoken, and shall he not make it good? Behold, I have received commandment to bless: and he hath blessed; and I cannot reverse it."

I said earlier, that any charge expressed, denotes the character and the intent of the one giving it. And so it is with Almighty God, for He shall never withdraw His gifts and blessings, although man, in his carnality, may squander or disregard them. But Almighty God, Who is immutable, shall never reverse or change His mind. His immutability then conveys to us His character and therefore His intent for man. *(cf. Heb. 13:8; James 1:17)* Moreover, a now word of faith regarding repentance, is often scorned because wisdom and knowledge is wanting within the carnal church consequently, many choke at the scant mention of it.

Meat in God's House

This revelation meat of repentance is given so that there would be meat in God's house! The question has been, "Where's the beef?" The answer should be found in God's house! However, due to an impoverished and sugar coated gospel message, congregations, across the board, are malnourished. **Truth #42: Christianity, a universal expression, does not absolve the saint of his duty to himself and of his obligation to God to repent, because a lifestyle of repentance is fatness to his soul!** Thus far repentance as the doctrine of God has been powerfully substantiated, but the question still remains, What does your conscience tell you? Have you been convinced of your carnality and self-righteousness? Do you still require more proof? Because if you do, there's plenty more ahead!

Chapter 6
Repentance in the Book of Deuteronomy

Repentance, Even in the Latter Days
Deuteronomy 4:29-31
*"But **if** from thence, thou shalt seek the Lord thy God, thou shalt find him, **if** thou shalt seek him with all thy heart and with all thy soul. When thou art in tribulation, and all these things are come upon thee, **even in the latter days, if** thou turn to the Lord thy God, and shalt be obedient unto his voice; (for the Lord thy God is a merciful God;) he will not forsake thee, nor forget the covenant of thy fathers, which he sware unto them." (cf. Matt. 4:17; Lk. 24:47)* (emphasis mine)

Moses spoke to the Israelites and said that if they were to seek the Lord their God, He would be found of them, providing of course that they sought Him with all their heart and soul. Notice that the heart is not the soul, yet is of the soul. The heart is the seat of the character of the soul and that of the individual. *(cf. Prov. 23:7; Matt. 15:18; Lk. 6:45)* Consequently, people are known by their character, for it is the disposition of their soul. Briefly stated, the soul consists of the mind, will and the emotions. It is from these that our character originates. Where character is an external mannerism, the soul is an internal function.

Verse 30, above implies that repentance shall exist even in the latter days. But in spite of this truth, there shall be those who will refuse to repent, even during the assault of God's wrath, as spoken of in the book of Revelations, and yet God shall send two witnesses who will exemplify repentance, even in sackcloth! *(cf. Rev. 11)*

To Remain Impenitent is to be Ignorant of Our Future
Deuteronomy 32:28-29, 36

"For they are a nation void of counsel, neither is there any understanding in them. O that they were wise, that they understood this, that they would consider their latter end! For the Lord shall judge his people, and repent himself for his servants, when he seeth that their power is gone, and there is none shut up or left."

Misguided faith and misunderstood repentance condemns humanity to the wrath of God! This is due to the fact that our mistaken interpretations of faith and of repentance are the cause of a broken covenant relationship and if faith is broken, God states that no faith exists. *(cf. Deut. 32:20, 51, AMP)* When we remain in our carnality, God repents on our behalf, because we won't consider our latter end. This sentiment is also found in the book of Haggai wherein at least four times, the prophet says to the people of his day, *"consider your ways."* **Truth #43: To remain unrepentant means to be ignorant of our future!** God repents on our behalf, much like a parent would suffer heartaches over their wayward child or their child who has fallen on difficult times. This was seen in the book of Exodus when, after four hundred years of bondage, God looked down and repented of himself on their behalf, that is too say, for their good!

Repentance Will Cause God to Rejoice Over Us for the Good
Deuteronomy 30:8-9

"And thou shalt return and obey the voice of the Lord, and do all his commandments which I command thee this day. And

the Lord thy God will make thee plenteous in every work of thy hand... for the Lord will again rejoice over thee for good, as he rejoiced over thy fathers:"

Truth #44: A lifestyle of repentance will draw God's good pleasure upon the saint! Through repentance, as that demonstration and qualification of faith, the saint invokes God's mercy, His goodness and favor; but without repentance, the saint negates the implementation of His blessings and the wrath of God is incurred. This must not be a burden that anyone should desire to shoulder.

Carnality as Dung/Putting On the Dog

Deuteronomy 23:12-14

"Thou shalt have a place also without the camp, whither thou shalt go forth abroad: And thou shalt have a paddle upon thy weapons; and it shall be, when thou shalt ease thyself abroad, thou shalt dig therewith, and shalt turn back and cover that which cometh from thee: For the Lord thy God walketh in the midst of thy camp, to deliver thee, and to give up thine enemies before thee; therefore shall thy camp be holy: that he see no unclean thing in thee, and turn away from thee."

In Philippians chapter 3 verses 1-8, Paul the Apostle, defamed his pedigree. Specifically in verse 8, Paul said that he counted all things [ambitions, confidences of the flesh, religious zeal] but loss, for the excellency of the knowledge of Christ and did count them but dung, that he may win Christ. What he meant was that his carnality exalted itself above the knowledge of God. (cf. 2 Cor. 10:4-6) It appears then, that Paul possessed a personal revelation about his own carnality and its spiritual counterpart, namely repentance. He said in Philippians chapter 3 verse 2 *"Beware of dogs..."* Paul, who was once a zealous pharisee, recognized the carnal dog within himself, for he saw the selfishness of the other pharisees.

The word dung as used in verse 8 means, *"refuse, that which is thrown to the dogs."* As far as God is concerned, man's carnality is table scraps, that which is eaten by dogs! But now Paul proclaimed that he no longer was the devil's pet, for he had received a revelation of the truth about his table scraps namely, his carnality. He renounced his pedigree saying in essence, that he threw it to the dogs, for he was made to see that all his pious, ceremonial, religious endeavors of carnality were the outward attempts of fleshly pursuits.

Such activity is a religious dress up and therefore is as putting on the dog. Carnality expressed, indicates a person's character has literally gone to the dogs. **Truth #45: Through a lifestyle of repentance, the saint no longer allows himself to remain as table scraps, as that which is thrown to the dogs. Neither is he putting on the dog of religious dress up!** The saint must no longer loaf about or shirk from his obligation to obey God's commands as a dog on the job! Sometime ago, while on a walk, a little stray, black dog crossed my path. Immediately, the Holy Ghost asked me this question. "Why is a dog known as man's best friend? The answer was simple enough. "Because it is!" Then He said, "The carnally minded man is his own best friend, for he too has put on the dog!"

The Dung Smear

Malachi 2:1-3

"And now, O ye priests, this commandment is for you. If ye will not hear, and if ye will not lay it to heart, to give glory unto my name, saith the Lord of Hosts, I will even send a curse upon you, and I will curse your blessings; yea, I have cursed them already, because you do not lay it to heart. Behold, I will corrupt your seed, and **spread dung upon your faces,** *even the dung of your solemn feasts; and one shall take you away with it." (cf. Isa. 36:12)* (emphasis mine)

Predatory animals will not eat the droppings from other animals. They will however, roll around in it, to conceal their own scent for the hunt. As a parallel to this fact, an actual incident occurred involving a municipal judge who smeared human excrement upon his face and body, as an illustration for this scriptural text. This officer of the court, practiced law during the day, but at night and on weekends would frequent massage houses in his particular locality where, in addition to the usual services rendered, he paid extra for the women to defecate on his chest! He then would smear this waste all over his face and chest! It just so happened, and unknown to this judge, that the local police department had this particular house under surveillance, which this judge did patronize. Eventually, a raid did take place. The parlor's cash and receipts and other items were taken as evidence, and the case was brought to trial. This judge, who was later disbarred, was sentenced to jail and registered as a sex deviate.

Another nefarious example of a reprobate mind is that of the infamous, cannibal, Jeffrey Dahmer, who butchered his victims and preserved their body parts on ice, only to be consumed later by him. Since all truth is parallel, it is evident that the extreme expressions and tendencies of carnality, reflects the Scripture, but also that of a dog!

Carnality, the Land Mines of the Soul

I find it rather odd that God's Word would even address a person's "business." I use to live in a nice trailer park south of Fort Worth, Texas. My next door neighbor owned a little dog and at least twice a day, she would walk her dog over to the grass area between our two trailers. My trailer was positioned offset from this grass area where this dog would do its business! It wasn't to long that these "land mines" became a real issue for me! You see, the main entrance to my trailer faced this grass and my driveway was adjacent to it. The odor, the flies, which were as big as *Chevys*, and the transition from green to brown were unbearable! I spoke to my neighbor three times about her discourtesy and inconsideration towards me, but she basically ignored everything I said. This was demonstrated by her circumvention of appropriate conduct and decent behavior. Although she ceased to walk her dog when I was home, she did continue to do so when I was out or after dark. I ended up calling the park management and the mess was cleaned up and the situation was resolved with a threat of her eviction.

As any land mine is an explosive device, these land mines left by her dog, were bonafide stink bombs and I didn't want to step in it! It is apparent then, that a person's conduct and behavior are indicative of the carnal land mines within their soul. These explosive devices of carnality, cause mayhem for others as well as for the individual, and yet, it doesn't have to be this way! The fact that her dog did its business, only reflects the filthy business of my neighbor's heart! **Truth #46: A lifestyle of repentance sanitizes one's soul effectively removing the filth, refuse and droppings left behind by iniquitous thoughts (lie-based-thinking!)**

Mind Your Own Business

But what does the Word of God have to say about such things? In Deuteronomy 23 Scripture indicates that God in fact does address this! From the place, to a hole and a shovel to cover, God commanded the people to mind their own business. There are dumping stations for R.V.s. There are public restrooms as well as the residential commode. Each facility is a separate place unto itself, which use is obvious.

Deuteronomy 23 verse 12, addressed a latrine. It was the place outside the camp. A latrine is a hole in the ground, that is dug proportionately depending on the size of the military encampment. Inside the camp, the soldier was protected, but outside the camp, he was exposed and vulnerable, literally with his pants down! Our carnality makes us exposed and vulnerable as well. **Truth #47: Through a lifestyle of repentance, the saint relieves himself of all the pressures of the flesh. He is protected from exposure and vulnerability, because through his lifestyle of repentance, (shovel, paddle) he minds his own business!**

A Shovel Among Your Weapons

A shovel comes in various shapes and sizes. From the handheld spade to the front end loader, from the plow to the grader, the application is the same. Even in the kitchen, a shovel's application is used to flip pancakes with a spatula, to scoop vegetables with a large spoon or to feed ourselves with a fork or spoon. 2 Corinthians chapter 10 verses 3 and 4 basically states that the saint's weapons are not carnal, but they are mighty through God even to the pulling down of strongholds. Ephesians chapter 6 verses 10 - 17 speaks of the armor of God, which the saint is to wear for battle. Isaiah chapter 54 verse 17 declares that no weapon formed against the saint shall prosper. And finally, Ecclesiastes chapter 9 verse 18 in part, states that wisdom is better than weapons of war!

With the exception of perhaps Ecclesiastes, the other Scriptures, are the most commonly known passages the traditional church is familiar with. But there is no mention of a shovel! Did Almighty God overlook the shovel? I think not, because He knew that there would be just a few resolute saints, with an excellent work ethic, to pick it up and have it upon their weapons. In light of this investigation, are you resolute to possess a shovel and to dig a ditch? **Truth #48: Whereas, a shovel is for digging and covering, a lifestyle of repentance is the means of excavation for the soul in and through which carnality is exposed. Repentance is also a covering to bury that which is as wastè matter of the carnal propensities! Truth #49: A lifestyle of repentance is the shovel long since neglected by the church, for the church fails to realize her need of the shovel called repentance!**

God Does Not Want to Step in It

Deuteronomy 23:14
"For the Lord thy God walks in the midst of thy camp...Therefore shall thy camp be holy..."

The saint of God must preserve the inward purity of his soul in consideration of the Holy Ghost Who occupies it. The filth of one's carnality is a noisome [nasty, foul, odious] pestilence to others in that it is injurious, harmful to health and is offensive to God. Such filth is an objective symptom of the offender's character. Just as you or I would avoid stepping in dog droppings, so will Almighty God avoid stepping in the refuse of our carnality! God does not want to step in it! He gave humanity a shovel called repentance. He expects us to carry it and to use it as necessary! Just as the disciples were instructed by Jesus to shake the dust from off their sandals and feet as a testimony against others who would not reciprocate their peace to them, likewise, God shall also shake man's carnal filth from his feet and sandals as a statement and a judgment against us! You see, man's carnality is the one thing that God does not want under His feet, because man's carnality is a stench to His nostrils and it's down right disrespectful and inconsiderate to boot! In other words, man's carnality is flatulence (fart), and as such carnality is a F.A.R.T. (Faithful Allegiance To Religious Traditions) and is therefore a stench to the nostrils!

Matthew 10:14 AMP
"And whoever will not receive and accept and welcome you nor listen to your message, as you leave that house or town, shake the dust [of it] from your feet." (cf. Mk. 6:11; Lk. 9:5)

Ephesians 1:22a
"And He has put all things under His feet...."

Times of War Should be Times of Reformation

In the foundational Scriptures of Deuteronomy pertaining to our text, it is evident that Almighty God spoke to the soldiers of the Hebrew encampment. He said that they were to have a shovel upon their weapons. The Israeli nation was birthed out of warfare and throughout their history, Israel has been seasoned and weathered by warfare even to this very day. Times of war should be times of reformation and the saints of God, like good soldiers, are to take care not to blow their cover. Morally, the saint must keep himself pure and his powder dry. He must remain unspotted from the accursed thing. He must take heed of his carnality, for this filth of his soul will erode his fighting edge for combat, rendering him a coward in the face of death or his enemy. However, the saint whose heart is pure and undefiled, has the courage and strength to confront his enemy as well as death so that, if necessary, he would die well as a martyr. Moral strength is superior to physical strength, just as wisdom is superior to weapons of war, for in it, are found the heart fibers of a godly character! **Truth #50: Whereas, physical strength is external and is often an audacious display of one's carnality, moral strength is that of the heart, for it is the internal function of holiness!**

Repentance as a Tool of the Trade

As a former California Highway Patrol Officer, I remember full well just how filthy I felt inwardly after a days work. It wasn't that I did anything evil or wrong, but because I had been exposed and made vulnerable to the dirt of public contact which always involved circumstances, situations, scenarios, I needed a bath! Under the color of authority, I became very polluted. As a road warrior, I had to wash my heart with God's Word of truth and regenerate my soul, for in bathing my soul, I found my time of refreshing. *(cf. Acts 3:19)* In effect, I had my shovel with me as a tool of my heart. Repentance therefore, is a tool of the trade, just as the equipment issued to me were tools of law enforcement. Without them, I could not perform my duties. Though I was armed to the teeth, without all my other equipment, I was incapable of doing my job. So it is for the saints of God. Though we may be adorned with the armor of God, without repentance, salvation is incomplete, because the saint is incapable of cultivating it.

The Proverb of the Shovel

Most would prefer to let another dig the ditch. To these, such back breaking work is beneath their dignity. They wouldn't dare blister the palm of their hands with such a menial task as ditch digging. Never mind the fact that to them, it's dirt cheap labor that should be left to the under achiever. The shovel, as a symbol of the blue collar cast system, is for most people, the lowest level of servitude. It's right down there with cleaning toilets! Shoveling is a thankless job, but somebody has to do it. Through repentance, the saints of God will be glad they did dig a ditch, for their eternal estate depends on their latrine! Repentance, although not necessarily a menial task, has been pigeonholed by church leadership, across the board, as just that, something beneath their dignity! Consequently for them, revival remains a wish and a hope. For the sake of the dignity of the pulpit, church leadership avoids the topic of repentance, because it's not fashionable to get down and dirty and yet that's exactly what revival entails!

The Shovel Known as Repentance

Truth #51: Repentance is a spiritual tool which the saint uses and the Holy Ghost employs to dig up, scoop away, turn over, bury, trench and grade the residue of iniquity within his soul! It's a work of righteousness and in this, the saint becomes a fellow worker with Christ, the very workmanship of God!

Jeremiah 1:10
"See, I have this day set thee over the nations and over the kingdoms, to root out, and to pull down, and to destroy, and to throw down, to build, and to plant."

2 Timothy 2:15
"Study to show thyself approved unto God, **a workman** that needeth not be ashamed, rightly dividing the word of truth." (cf. 1 Cor. 3:9; 15:58) (emphasis mine)

Philippians 2:12b AMP
"...work out (**cultivate, carry out** to the goal, and fully complete) your own salvation with reverence and awe and trembling (**self distrust, with serious caution**, tenderness of conscience, watchfulness under temptation, timidly shrinking from whatever might offend God and discredit the name of Christ)." (emphasis mine)

Without the excavation of one's carnality from within the soul, salvation is not consummated and therefore shall not exist, because that which makes one wise unto salvation does not exist. It's breaking faith and if faith is broken, then faith does not really exist! **Truth #52: The shovel of repentance is the tool by which carnality is expunged from the soul and salvation is cultivated in the heart!**

The Reason and the Purpose

There is a reason and a purpose for everything. The shovel's purpose is to dig the dirt. Without the dirt, there's no need or reason for the shovel. Therefore, the reason for dirt, precedes the shovel's purpose. The reason the addict endures withdrawal symptoms is due to his bodies purpose for expunging itself of the contaminants put into it. Likewise, the purpose of repentance is to expunge the reason for it. That reason is the dirt of carnality.

Without carnality, there would be no need for repentance. Like the withdrawal symptoms the addict endures, man's carnality is a regression from holiness, because these carnal withdrawal symptoms denote the soul's need for purity and the heart's need for righteousness. The body, therefore must purge these impurities, for its need of cleanliness. Our bodies were created for the good and pure, and not for the bad and the polluted. **Truth #53: The reason carnality exists is to reveal the need/purpose for repentance, for without the dirt, there is no need for the shovel!**

Before the Well, There was the Shovel

Before the well, there was a shovel. The purpose for the shovel therefore, is to dig the well for the singular reason, people need to drink water. The shovel of repentance was given for the sole purpose to first dig the well, for without the shovel, the well could not exist. Therefore, repentance is the shovel by which the saint digs the well of salvation, from which the life giving waters of regeneration are drawn. *(cf. Is. 12:3; Titus 3:5)* Too many churches are wells without water. They have become complacent with this tool of the trade and accordingly have lost their proficiency, because they failed to have a shovel with their weapons! Where they should be salvation respites, through drought and famine, they have become tombs and graveyards for the dead and the dying of thirst and malnutrition! *(cf. 2 Pet. 2:12-17)* This present condition of malnourishment and inefficiency is a railing indictment to the effects of churchianity, religion, pride, passivity and the ignorance of man!

Matthew 5:6
"Blessed are they who do hunger and thirst after righteousness, for they shall be filled."

Chapter 7
Repentance in the Book of Joshua

Joshua 7:1, 11, 13
"But the children of Israel committed a trespass in the accursed thing: for A'chan, the son of Car'mi....of the tribe of Judah, took of the accursed thing: and the anger of the Lord was kindled against the children of Israel. Israel hath sinned, and they have also transgressed my covenant which I commanded them: for they have taken of the accursed thing, and have also stolen, and dissembled [hypocrisy, pretense] also, and they have put it even among their own stuff. Up, sanctify the people, and say, Sanctify yourselves against to morrow, for thus saith the Lord God of Israel, **There is an accursed thing in the midst of thee,** *O Israel: thou canst not stand before thine enemies, until ye take away the accursed thing from among you."* (emphasis and brackets mine)

Impressions of Deception

Human frailties are character flaws. They are impressions of deception which are the outward expressions of conduct and behavior. These character flaws are lodged within man's carnality. It has been said, that no man is an island, but in chapter 7, we learn that one man's short coming did effect an entire nation! In fact, thirty-six men where killed, because of one man's careless gesture of covetousness. This act of deprecation was the dung smear of A'chan's self indulgence. He was a stingy, little man on the back side of the desert! He betrayed his own people, with this one act of selfishness, which imperiled the lives of thirty-six honorable men and that of his entire family. *(verses 16-26)* With the nation at war, Joshua did not need some fool to evince his defiance behind his back, for such unsolicited conduct and behavior only served to undermine his authority and the morale of the people! Verse 13 states, *"...there is an accursed thing in the midst of thee!"* Since no one else knew of this accursed thing within the camp, Almighty God had to inform Joshua of its existence. As it was then, so it still remains, people today must be made aware of the accursed carnality in the midst of them! Unless carnality is exposed for what and where it is, people will be unable to stand up against it and defeat the selfish propensities resident within their souls. A'chan's selfishness was an outward expression, caused by the inward deception of his own carnality. A'chan was a thief, and was found guilty of the crime of shoplifting. His rapacity [greed] was more important than his family, the slain warriors and Joshua's trust! A'chan, like a little child who stole from the store shelf, was soon caught after the fact. **Truth #54: Through a lifestyle of repentance, the little child named carnality, is found out and punished, for it is the accursed thing!**

Finally, Somebody Caught the Revelation

In verse 26, the Bible states that Joshua and his people heaped a pile of stones as a memorial to A'chan's theft in the valley of A'chor. Finally, somebody caught the revelation of the destructive tendencies of carnality! When these stones were heaped together, God lifted His wrath. The point being, God commands His people today, to acquire carnal knowledge, for the knowledge of their carnality is an abhorrent eulogy of the ever present propensities of their iniquity! Once this knowledge is acquired, then people can deal responsibly with sin.

As an illustration of repentance, we must remember that just as our carnality effects those about us, likewise repentance has a positive influence upon others as well. Where the one is an evil activity and a work of the flesh as selfishness, the latter is an lifestyle and work of God's righteousness. This is seen in verse 6, when upon learning of the slain warriors and the accursed thing within the camp, Joshua rent [tore] his garments in utter dismay, and with the elders about him, fell to the ground, face down until the evening, putting the dust of the earth upon their heads. This act of intercession was the key that unlocked the word of knowledge, vital to the encampment, for without it, God's wrath would not have been stayed. **Truth #55: Through a lifestyle of repentance, God's wrath is stayed, because the saint has acquired carnal knowledge by which he is able to suppress the insurgency within his soul!**

Something Sinister

Joshua believed every word [promise] Moses had uttered. Joshua saw the mighty hand of God liberate the Hebrews from Egyptian bondage and the provision created to sustain them. Joshua had no reason to doubt God or Moses because he knew, first hand, of the many supernatural interventions. But now, things were different. Moses is dead and something was wrong! Something sinister was lurking about and Joshua didn't have a clue, until... he did repentance before God. Joshua remembered Moses falling prostrate before God in the presence of the murmuring horde, as he interceded on their behalf and like Moses, Joshua knew these people. He knew what made them tick. He knew their pulse. To Joshua, his leadership was not just a job for God, but too say the very least, it was an adventure! Joshua, like Moses, was not a hireling, for he did not run off leaving the people without a leader. He, like Moses, was a true shepherd! Would to God, that existing leadership would never cower away as they do and that they too would come to know their people as

Joshua and Moses did! Joshua also knew, most importantly, that the promises of God were promises kept, because God is not a man that He would lie, nor the son of man that He should repent.

The A'chan Factor and the Accursed Thing

What becomes an accursed thing to man, in his carnality, is a consecrated thing to God, spiritually! We saw this with what happened to Korah and the two hundred fifty censers, in chapter 5 of this work. *(cf. Joshua 6:18-19)* Romans 11:29 tells us that the gifts and callings of God are without repentance. This means that every person was given, has been given, and shall be given gifts, talents and abilities, whose sole purpose is to glorify Almighty God, the gift giver! Whenever man fails to give glory and honor to God in and through these consecrated things, man, because of his carnality, allows these consecrated things to become accursed, for he has stolen from God by catering to the selfish desires of his flesh, rather than fulfill the desires of God's pleasure! **Truth #56: Through a lifestyle of repentance, the saint of God unearths his carnality, and as an act of discovery, reveals that which is holy before the Lord and destroys the accursed carnality within him!**

Chapter 8
Repentance in the Book of Judges

To Judge is to Self Examine
Judges 2:1b-2, 18
*"...but I will never break my covenant with you. And ye shall make no league with the inhabitants of this land; ye shall throw down their altars: but ye have not obeyed my voice: **why have ye done this?**" ...And when the Lord raised up judges, then the Lord was with the Judge, and delivered them out of the hand of their enemies all the days of the judge: for it repented the Lord because of their groanings by reason of them that oppressed them and vexed them."* (emphasis mine)

It was bad enough that the Israelis where in Egyptian bondage for four hundred years, decades earlier; yet in the book of Judges, and according to the historical time line, the Israelis found themselves back in oppressive bondage again, but this time under the rule of the Midianites, Ammonites, Philistines, etc. and for another four hundred fifty years! This was due, once again, to their long standing disobedience, for everyone did what was right in their own eyes. *(cf. Jdg. 2:10-13, 8:33-35)* In verse 18, we learn that without a judge, the Israelis would have no means to facilitate God's doctrine of repentance, as it related to the Old Testament offerings. This implied that with the providentially appointed judge, the people could comply to God's laws and He would receive their oblations. God was with the judge and delivered the Israelis from their enemies, for without the judge, they would be lost. Likewise, we are to judge ourselves in the light of Scripture, for without God's Word, we too are lost. Once our days are over, Jesus Christ, the Great High Priest and Judge of all, shall either sentence us to eternal death or to eternal life. Either way, the sentence received is a judgment rendered, based upon the evidence of our living, but afterwards shall be the result of the sowing and reaping in our lives, now.

2 Corinthians 13:5
"Examine yourselves, whether ye be in the faith, prove your own selves..." (cf. 1 Cor. 11:28)

Isaiah 26:9b
"...for when thy judgments are in the earth, the inhabitants of the earth will learn righteousness."

Again, verse 18 states, *"And when the Lord raised them up judges, then the Lord was with the judge and delivered them out of their groanings..."* Again, the word of God states in 1 Corinthians 2:15, *"...The spiritual man judges all things, yet he, himself is judged of no man."* **Truth #57: Repentance then, is a personal assessment of the saint's obedience to the word of faith and to the word of God's righteousness!**

I Don't Know!

Almighty God asked this question of them, *"Why have you done this?"* Their initial answer might have been, "We don't know!" In reflection, how many times have parents asked their children this very same question, only to be told, "I don't know!" Of course the kids don't know! How could they, at their young age. Sadly though, there are adults who don't know either! How many times does a patient tell his psychologist, "I don't know?" I remember as a child, I had often asked my dad, why this or why that. His reply was, "Gee son, I don't know. Go ask your mother!" Well, his ignorance was a big disappointment to me. Soon, I stopped asking my dad anything, because he didn't know! God wants us to know why we do things and that His word contains the answer. This wisdom and revelation is, for the saints of God, specific, working knowledge of carnality, of salvation and of the knowledge of Jesus Christ. *(cf. 2 Cor. 7:8-10; Eph.1:17-18; Phil. 2:12)* Therefore, repentance is useless, without knowing why we do things!

Repentance must have a destination and our faith should provide the direction. *(cf. Acts 20:21)* It could be said that faith is the candy that makes the medicine of repentance easy to swallow. **Truth #58: Without the knowledge of salvation, as carnal knowledge, a lifestyle of repentance is a waste of time!** Faith in God assures us that He does exist. Without faith, a person basically rejects the existence of the one, true God and settles for a "higher power" which could be anything in their estimation. Should God be rejected, then there is no need to know why we do the things that we do, nor is there a need to repent, since repentance must have a destination in Almighty God!

A Crisis Intervention Technique

Judges 21:6, 15

"And the children of Israel repented them for Benjamin their brother, and said, There is one tribe cut off from Israel this day. And the people repented them for Benjamin, because the Lord had made a breach in the tribes of Israel."

The word, *repented* as used in these two verses means, "compassion." It relates to the homosexual activity and the dismemberment of a woman, who was killed by the reprobates in chapter 19:22-30. Repentance deals with the problem, having compassion for the person. **Truth #59: Through a lifestyle of**

repentance, the saint deals with the carnal problem first, but has compassion for the person. Repentance therefore involves the restoration of one's position and possession! Repentance then is a crisis intervention technique, because the problem is attacked first, and an assault on the individual is avoided. When you think of it, Jesus Christ dealt with the sin problem on the cross of Calvary, did He not? Through faith in His blood, the sin element has already been dealt with by God, Himself. All the saint must do is appropriate the provisions of salvation. Freedom from the bondage of sin is extended to whosoever will. Truly, if there ever was a life and death crisis, the state of our eternal soul is one!

Chapter 9
Repentance in the Book of Ruth

Origin of Incest

Moab was the son of Lot through an incestuous union between one of Lot's two daughters and himself. *(cf. Gen. 19:37-38)* Six centuries later, Ruth was born as Lot's great grand daughter, and as a Moabite, she was a gentile. The word, *Moabite* comes from the root word, *Moab* which means, "of the father." Hence, Moab was the father of the Moabites. (Strong's Exhaustive Concordance; Heb. Ref.# 4124, page 62) Lot's younger daughter also bore a son whom she named, *Ben-ammi* which means "son of my people." He became the father of the Ammonites, which is now the capital city of Jordan. Both tribes populated Jordan. They were relatives to each other and cousin to the Israelites, even to this very day! (Baker Encyclopedia, page 25)

Carnal Progeny

Genesis 19:31-32
"Our father is aging and there is not a man on earth to live with us in the customary way. Come let us make our father drunk with wine and we will lie with him, so that we may preserve offspring [our race] through our father."

Nearly six centuries earlier, as Genesis 16 shows, Sarai, Abraham's barren wife, suggested to him to take Hagar, her Egyptian maid, and bare a son with her. This union produced Ishmael, whose descendants fought against they of Isaac's [Israel] lineage. However, here in chapter 4, Boaz, as a righteous man, stated, *"...for there is none to redeem it besides thee, and I am after thee... to raise up the name of the dead upon his inheritance."* His priorities were correct and his integrity was above reproach, for he was an upright man before the Lord his God. Considering these three accounts objectively, a contrast appears between Lot's two daughters, Sarai, Abraham's wife and Boaz. Where the first two were motivated by the self-indulgence of their carnality, and subsequently were enslaved by the law of sin and death, Boaz was provoked to godliness by his upright spirit and that of the law of the Spirit of life.

Although there are various factors involved with each historical account, there is a similarity, with each account; it's kinsmanship! Each account involved a posterity [progeny] issue, either of race or the propagation of a name. In Ruth chapter 4 however, Boaz's unidentified, older brother refused to redeem the inheritance, which belonged to his older brother Elimelech, Naomi's dead husband, because he was already married. *(cf. Ruth 1:3)* Furthermore, chapter 4 introduces the laws of estate, which pertained to the redemption and exchange of properties and assets from the deceased to the surviving family members or other benefactors, so designated. *(cf. Heb. 9:16-17)* These assets had to be lawfully pursued by Boaz, and being a law abiding citizen, he did not hesitate to do just that. *(cf. Rom. 7:1; 1 Cor. 14:40)*

The Caste System

Another word for estate is *stratification*, which implies a three fold classification of society. These three categories are commonly known as the "Caste System." The three classes are 1) The *Caste* category which includes people of servitude. These remain subservient all their lives. They are born into servitude and they die in it, with no hope of expecting anything more out of life. 2) *Estate* category, refers to the exceptional few who move vertically (upward mobility, promotion) in life. 3) *Class* category, implies that everyone has the right to enter the race for advancement, and most do, thereby exchanging their position and condition in their lives. (The Volume Library, page 2000, col. A and C) The spiritual import being that when a person comes to faith in Jesus Christ, through God's mercy and grace, the new convert is vertically challenged, from a posture of servitude to his carnality, to possessing an eye to serve the Living God, which is that higher call! Therefore, a lifestyle of repentance secures this higher call, for repentance qualifies the saint's promotion and ultimate redemption! *(cf. Matt. 6:24)* As law abiding citizens of heaven, we should remember the terms and conditions of God's covenant. What is real in the union between Christ and His people, becomes the foundation of what is legal, and saving faith is that bond which satisfies the divine contract!

Repentance Given to the Gentiles

Acts 5:31 teaches that repentance was granted to the gentiles, and since it was granted, then it is also a gift! Ruth was a gentile and Boaz was a portrait of Jesus Christ. He purchased his deceased brother's inheritance as well as Ruth. *(cf. Lk. 20:27-38)* It could be said that the inheritance came with the package, Ruth! In other words, when Jesus Christ becomes Lord to the saint, then all the provisions of God's grace automatically and legally belongs to the saint!

This legal transaction of exchange benefited Naomi and Ruth alike, in that they were immediately promoted according to estate law, in their living condition and position. A purchase was forfeited by one and a price was paid by another, thereby making the right of redemption secure. Boaz raised up the name (of righteousness) upon the inheritance of God's chosen people,

His elect. Likewise, through Jesus Christ, God's redemption is upon the inheritance, found in and of the saints!

A Method of Operation

Practically any man or woman may bring a child into this world. But to raise up that child, as a member of the family so that he/she obtains a goodly character and becomes an asset to society, will require the parents to embark on a lifelong journey to train up that child. Therefore, proper rearing is compulsory as an adopted method of operation, which would lead toward spiritual training. Such training should be that of godliness! *(cf. Prov. 22:6; 2 Cor. 7:8, 11, 13; 1 Tim. 4:7-8)* **Truth #60: A lifestyle of repentance involves the adopted method of the operation of God's righteousness at work within the soul, for it is a lifelong journey to discipline the soul against carnality!** I say adopted, because repentance requires an abrupt adjustment in life. A lifestyle of repentance is a necessary work ethic, because it is spiritual training that leads to godliness. After a child is brought into the world, the parents must adjust their lives to accommodate the new life and addition to their family. As the book of Proverbs instructs us to train up a child in the way that he should go, these parents are obligated to God, to society and to the child to comply, and just as any child is innately selfish, the parents must train the child to overcome and, if possible, to out grow this childish tendency. **Truth #61: Through a lifestyle of repentance, the saint, like a parent, trains the little child within his soul, whose name is carnality, to behave! Otherwise, a childish character flaw entrenches itself within the soul of the adult.**

In the psychological field, doctors introduce their patients to their "little child" within. This child, although an apparent psychological tendency within the mind of the patient, could be considered the source of their dysfunctions. This child belongs to their past, and as such, is the source of many dysfunctional propensities. **Truth #62: Man's carnality is that little child within the soul and must be disciplined and suppressed!** This child must be made to go to its room! An adult may think that a child should be seen and not heard; yet when it comes to man's carnality, a lifestyle of repentance will confront carnality and expose its selfish or childish propensities!

Progeny Means Fruit

Progeny means "fruit" among other things. Boaz demonstrated the fruit of his righteous character when he redeemed Ruth. The inheritance, which consisted of property or land, was secondary to Ruth and God's continuing plan of redemption for all humanity. As husband and wife, Boaz and Ruth became the progenitors of the righteous lineage to King David and to Jesus, the Christ! *(cf. Ruth 4:18-22; Matt.1:5-18)* **Truth #63: Through a lifestyle of repentance, the saint brings forth fruits of repentance, as he redeems his soul from the ravages of his carnality!** *(cf. Matt. 3:8)*

The Progeny of Repentance

The word, progenitive is an adjective and as such its use is to modify a noun. In this sense, it implies a process of regeneration, reconstruction, reformation or recreation. (Webster's) **Truth #64: A lifestyle of repentance is therefore, progenitive in that regeneration, reconstruction, reformation and reconciliation of the saint's condition, in his carnality, has begun, for he has positioned himself to be a recipient of Christ's redemption!** In this, Christ becomes his Kinsman Redeemer who has purchased the saint's salvation. Therefore, salvation is maintained through the progenitive qualities of the word of His righteousness! *(cf. Titus 3:5; James 1:21)*

Notes:

Chapter 10

Repentance in the Book of 1ˢᵗ Samuel

1 Samuel 15:22-29, 35
"And Samuel said, hath the Lord **as great** delight in burnt offerings and sacrifices, as in obeying the voice of the Lord? Behold, to obey is better than sacrifice, and to hearken better than the fat of rams. For rebellion is as the sin of witchcraft, and stubbornness is as iniquity and idolatry. Because thou has rejected the word of the Lord, he hath also rejected thee from being king. And Saul said unto Samuel, I have sinned: for I have transgressed the commandment of the Lord, and thy words: because I feared the people, and obeyed their voice. Now, therefore, I pray thee, pardon my sin, and turn again with me, that I may worship the Lord. And Samuel said unto Saul, I will not return with thee: for thou hast rejected the word of the Lord, and the Lord hast rejected thee from being king over Israel. And as Samuel turned about to go away, he laid hold upon the skirt of his mantle, and rent it. And Samuel said unto him, The Lord hath rent the kingdom of Israel from thee this day, and hath given it to a neighbor of thine, **that is better than thou.** And also, the Strength of Israel will not lie nor repent for he is not a man that he should repent.... And Samuel came no more to see Saul until the day of his death: nevertheless, Samuel mourned for Saul: and the Lord repented that he had made Saul king over Israel." (emphasis mine)

The Mantle of Repentance

God's voice to us is His Word to us! There is a cloak of humility and a mantle of repentance that the saints of God are to adorn. To tear the mantle of repentance, as King Saul did, is to reject the requirements of godliness and holiness! Let each saint purpose within his heart to wear the mantle of repentance, for in doing so, he decks himself with majesty and excellency, because he has arrayed himself with glory and beauty! *(cf. Job 40:9-10)* Like the high priest who wore the breastplate of judgment over the ephod, or like the sackcloth worn by the penitent Jew, a lifestyle of repentance must be adorned by the penitent saint. **Truth #65: A lifestyle of repentance means that the saint must wear the mantle of repentance over a cloak of humility!** Otherwise, the saint retains his stubbornness and he affirms his iniquity. However, through a lifestyle of repentance, he disrobes them before God.

Psalm 38:17-18 AMP
"For I am ready to halt and fall: my pain and sorrow are continually before me. For I do confess my guilt and iniquity; I am filled with sorrow for my sin."

Job 42:5-6 AMP
"I had heard of you [only] by the hearing of the ear, but now my [spiritual] eyes see you. Therefore I loathe [my words] and abhor myself and repent in dust and ashes."

The Oil and the Wine

Do you suppose the gentility of all politicians have repented themselves of their corrupt politics and have declared their iniquity? Revelation chapter 6 verse 6 basically states that the ruling politic was not to hurt the oil and the wine. The oil and wine speaks of currency and the economy of the nations. Presently, the United States is at war with Iraq. French wine has been boycotted by Americans, due to that nations presidential antagonism against the American war effort. Although their defiant antagonism has been marshaled against us, the real issue is not so much our war effort, but the billions of dollars in economic trade which France, along with a few other nations, have with Iraq's dictator, Saddam Hussein! When his regime is overthrown, all the contracts between these nations and Iraq will be rendered null and void. France especially, could care less about the loss of human life in Iraq, because of her greed. These nations, that have entered into these unauthorized contractual agreements, have defied the United Nations sanctions, prohibiting Iraq from any commerce with other countries. It's been reported that each of these nations had stipulated to Iraq, that no terrorist activity would be committed on their soil! As long as the genocide remains in Iraq, and terrorism occurs elsewhere, these blackmailed nations would continue to support Saddam, for the sake of their own economy. And as long as their economy is strong or the citizens believe it to be so, these ruling despots can do whatever they want and get away with it! Do you suppose that Saddam Hussein is truly sorry for his tyranny? Do you suppose, when cornered and with no avenue of escape, that this reprobate will be remorseful for his atrocities just because he was caught, captured and brought to charges? A rat in a trap is still a rat. It may squeal when caught, but it's still vermin. Like King Saul, an unrepentant heart is a tormented soul, entertaining evil influences.

The Iniquity of Stubbornness

1 Samuel 15:23
"...stubbornness is as iniquity and idolatry. Because thou hast rejected the word of the Lord.

Stubbornness, as an iniquity, is a toxic poison of the unrenewed mind and within the unregenerate soul. Stubbornness is mulishness due to ignorance. It's one thing to be ignorant as a result of circumstances beyond one's control, but to remain ignorant, when the opportunities to mature present themselves, is down right stupid! Mule-headed people are ignorant of their own ignorance, because they frustrate God's grace! Such carnal tendencies are also found in leadership positions, from the podium to the pulpit!

Jeremiah 10:14
"Every man is brutish in his own knowledge..."

Jeremiah 10:21
"For the pastors have become brutish and have not sought the Lord: therefore they shall not prosper, and all their flocks shall be scattered."

Jeremiah 10:23
"O Lord, I know that the way of man is not in himself, it is not in man that walketh to direct his steps."

Whenever a man remains mule-headed, in the ignorance of his carnality, he stays calloused towards the spiritual things of God, and as any mule is a beast of burden, so too then shall this man remain burdened by the weight of the sin that so easily besets him! *(cf. Heb 12:1)* Why? Because stubbornness is an iniquity, which is part and parcel to carnality and is therefore idolatry, for it knows no denominational or ethnic barriers! The person who doggedly worships his own obstinance and traditions, no matter what the facts or truths may say to the contrary, this man is idolatrous in his iniquity and is therefore practicing witchcraft!

The "Yada, Yada, Yada" of "Yea But"

Traditionally, as a right of conquest, the conquering warrior would take the very best of his enemies spoils and keep them for himself. However, King Saul was instructed to destroy all the people, all the sheep and all the oxen. He was not to take anything for himself! But, he didn't. In fact, he partially obeyed! However, in his attempt to circumvent Samuel's instructions to him, Saul was also completely disobedient. As saints of God, we must realize that to acquire the virtue of a godly character, our complete and total obedience to the terms and conditions of God's word is essential, for partial obedience is no different than complete disobedience. This is because partial obedience is an abuse of truth, since it skirts the moral law found in God's word. When a man is partially obedient, his disobedience shows that he has no due diligence towards a excellent character of godliness! *(cf. Lev. 5:18; Phil. 4:8)* As they say, "Yada, Yada, Yada...."

The fact that King Saul chose to conceal the sheep, which he was to destroy represented a "Yea but," which was an objective symptom of his carnality. Have you ever said that yourself? No matter what truth or evidence might have been presented to you, as a contradiction to a particular issue you were partial too, you thought or said, "Yea but...." This defensive statement essentially annulled the relevance of the truth or evidence presented, and in so doing, you qualified yourself for the opposing intention. *But*, cancels out all previous conditions. *But*, is the antithesis and it qualifies a person to their particular mind set. "Yea but," is carnal mindedness and "But God," is spiritual mindedness. Where the former is death, the latter is righteousness, peace and joy in the Holy Ghost. *(cf. Rom. 14:17)*

Scripture is replete with the word, *but*. However, to properly assimilate this powerful truth, it is important to comply with the laws of language and interpretation. *Estoppel* therefore, is another legal term used by attorneys. It means, "the barring of a person, in legal proceeding, from making allegations or denials which are contrary to either a previous statement or act by that person or a previous adjudication."(Webster's) In effect, this stipulation prevents a person from reneging on a statement or act previously made. Applied to the use of the word *but* in Scripture, then it is evident that *but*, is a word used to renege on the terms and conditions of a covenant. When impenitent humanity stands before a just and righteous God, they shall know that they will have no legal claim or excuse for their breach of covenant as they lived on earth; and there will be no reneging of any statement or act made by them, as they lived. To the contrary, the preponderance of evidence which Almighty God shall exhibit, as a statement against them, shall prevent this denial.

Legal Claims

Romans 7:1 AMP
"Do you not know, brethren-for I am speaking to men who are acquainted with the Law-that legal claims have power over a person only for as long as he is alive?"

God's Word establishes the principles of all legal claims in life. Therefore, spoken words must be carefully uttered. *But*, will either cancel out a truth or, by opportunity, lay a foundation for another truth, believed. *(cf. Mk. 11:22-24; Prov. 6:2; Matt. 12:34-37)*

Romans 7:8
"...but sin, finding opportunity in the commandment..."

Romans 7:11-13
"For sin, seizing the opportunity by taking its incentive from the commandment and using it as a weapon to kill me...It was sin, working death in me by using this good thing [commandment] as a weapon..."

Aside from the natural speech organ, there is another tongue hidden and yet very apparent to any individual. The *soliloquy* of self deception is a common trait of carnal thinking. It means to self talk oneself into. Therefore, the silent tongue of the unregenerate soul and the unrenewed mind is a hidden member of the conscience, which must be tamed! Either way, whatever truth one chooses to live by, that truth is a legal claim mandated by the individual.

James 3:6 AMP
"And the tongue is a fire. [The tongue is a] world of wickedness set among our members, contaminating and depraving the whole body and setting on fire the wheel of birth (the cycle of man's nature), being itself ignited by hell (Gehenna)."

Romans 8:5-10
"For they that are after the flesh do mind the things of the flesh; ***but*** *they that are after the Spirit the things of the Spirit. For to be carnally minded is death,* ***but*** *to be spiritually minded is life and peace. Because the carnal mind is enmity against God: for it is not subject to the law of God, neither indeed can be. So then they that are in the flesh can not please God.* ***But*** *ye are not in the flesh,* ***but*** *in the Spirit, if so be that the Spirit of God dwell in you. Now if any man have not the Spirit of Christ, he is none of his. And if Christ be you, the body is dead because of sin,* ***but*** *the Spirit is life because of righteousness."* (emphasis mine)

Illustrated "Buts"

The mind is not the brain. Where the brain is an organ of the anatomy, the mind is the psyche of the soul. The mind is psycho graphic, in that it has the ability to project images within the theater of its intelligence, and depending on the intellect, its capability to project imagery is hinged to the experience and the knowledge of the individual. In other words, a person who is void of a greater mental dimension and capacity would be restricted in his ability to picture things in the theater of his mind, thereby making apprehension or comprehension of spiritual truths more difficult. It is similar to the varying speeds and powers of microprocessors that are found in computers, as these determine the capability of the computer. The greater the capacity, the greater the function and versatility. The lower the capacity, the more restrictive the function and versatility. However, the mind that is expanded would have little or no difficulty in grasping a new concept or idea. It's been said, that our thoughts are things. That's because we all think in pictures. The imagery of the mind, enables us to picture things in the eye of reason without the use of our natural eye sight. Otherwise, it would be impossible to define or to describe anything. Therefore, the following word pictures are given to illustrate the spiritual truth of "but." Scripture abounds with illustrations, as any concordance would reveal.

1. *But* is a switchback upon the slope of a mountain, *for its many turns*. As soon as a driver heads in the one direction, suddenly, he must turn in the opposite! This switching occurs repeatedly while en route to a destination, only to be repeated again, on the return trip!

2. *But* is like an amusement park's staging area *for its many turns*, wherein exists parallel bars, chains or ropes, as lanes, so as to condense as many people in as little space as possible.

3. *But* is a snakes slither, *for its many turns*, which may be seen tracking across a dirt trail. The evidence of it is found in Scripture as well. Just as the serpent beguiled man with his undulating tactics of deceit, throughout history, likewise, God's Word of truth has a raised serpent, as that standard of righteousness, to remedy satanic and carnal devices! *(cf. Gen. 3:1-7; Num. 21:6-9)*

4. Laughter as scorn, is a "Yea but." for it denies God's Word. God desires that His saints be impregnated with His Word! Where most seem to have given birth to a religious *Ishmael*,

whose name means, "God will hear." a remnant have given birth to a righteous *Isaac*, whose name means "laughter." *(cf. Gen. 18:15, 21:1-6; Rom. 1:21-27, 32, 2:5, 4:19-20)* The joy of the Lord is to be our strength, and holy laughter, like medicine, accompanies this power. Therefore, the saints of God have the last laugh in and through a lifestyle of repentance! **Truth #66: A lifestyle of repentance is a switchback, for its many turns to the saint's carnal mind, and its evidence is seen as the standard of righteousness that is raised against carnal devices!**

Proverbs 12:25
"Anxiety in a man's heart weighs it down, but an encouraging word makes it glad."

Proverbs 15:13
"A glad heart makes a cheerful countenance, but by sorrow of the heart, my spirit is broken."

Proverbs 15:15 AMP
"All the days of the desponding and the afflicted are made evil [by anxious thoughts and forebodings], but he who has a glad heart has a continual feast [regardless of circumstances]."

Proverbs 17:22
"A merry heart is good medicine and a cheerful mind works and promotes healing, but a broken spirit dries the bones."

Proverbs 18:14
"The strong spirit of a man sustains him in bodily pain or trouble, but a weak and broken spirit, who can bare?"

Isaiah 57:16
"For I will not contend forever, neither will I be angry always

[for if I did stay angry] the spirit of man would faint and be consumed before me and my purpose in creating the souls of men would be frustrated."

Psalm 107:17-20
"Some are fools [made ill] because of the way of their transgressions and are afflicted because of their iniquities. They loathe every kind of food, and they draw near to the gates of death. Then they cry to the Lord in their trouble, and he delivers them out of their distresses. He sends forth his word and heals and rescues them form the pit and destruction."

Job 21:23-26
"One dies in his full strength, being wholly at ease and quiet; his pails are full of milk [his veins are filled with nourishment], and the marrow of his bones is fresh and moist, Whereas another man dies in bitterness of soul and never tastes of pleasure or good fortune. They lie down alike in the dust, and the worm spreads a covering over them." (cf. Lev. 17:11; 1 Cor. 11:26-30)

Chapter 11
Repentance in the Book of 2nd Samuel

Repentance Must Cost Something

This book continues the history of the establishment of David's kingdom. Two events in David's life come to mind. The first was his adulterous relationship with Bathsheba, involving the murder of Uriah, the Hittite, the husband to Bathsheba. The other was the occasion of David numbering the people. Specifically, in 2 Samuel 11:1-17, we read of this first account. Uriah was a more honorable man drunk, than David was sober! Where Uriah was intoxicated with wine, David was besotted with his carnality! Uriah refused to accept the creature comforts of a good night's sleep at home and the conjugal pleasures with his wife, while his army was out on the front lines of battle. Uriah counted the cost of the delights of creature comforts, because he was a seasoned, battle hardened warrior. His motivation was his strength and honor as a valiant soldier. Although he was eventually betrayed by his commander, Uriah fought to the very end without question. **Truth #67: A lifestyle of repentance then is the ongoing activity of taking the proper assessment of life, by keeping first things first, between creature comforts and spiritual integrity!** In short, Uriah counted the cost of compromise! David however, paid the price of his carnality!

Truth or Consequences

In 2nd Samuel chapter 24 verses 1-9, we read that David

numbered the people. Verse 10 shows that David's heart did smite him. Have you ever felt a gnawing, gut wrenching prod, deep within that convinced you that you just made a bad mistake? Well seemingly, this is what David experienced. There are two game shows called, "Jeopardy" and "Truth of Consequences" whose hosts present a problem to the contestants and depending on their answer, the contestants are awarded the truth or the consequence [risk] of their decision. Similarly, a more recent game show called, "Who wants to be a Millionaire?" is also based upon the "final answer." The answer given will either increase or decrease the reward money and the contestant is permitted to walk away with his judgment. It seems then, that truth or consequences are accepted in game shows, and yet the truth or consequences of life apparently are overlooked. Could it be that most people consider life a game? Could it be that most church goers consider their relationship with God a big joke or a wager, as they gamble their salvation? Could it be that most people live their lives out of self gratuities, having little or no regard for the painful consequence?

Foolishness is Carnality

David said to the Prophet Gad, that he had sinned. *(24:14)* He immediately repented of his sin and acknowledged that his foolishness was a propensity of his carnality! When man persistently follows through with his impulsive indulgences, he too is foolish before the eyes of God. Such strongholds represent character flaws in our living. Although God is merciful and full of grace, He will never condone the self indulgences which we allow to reside in our hearts! God shall continue to extend His mighty hand towards humanity, but it is the responsibility of each person and nationality to accept His help no matter how painful His remedy might become. Otherwise, our doom is the consequence of our decision, because the choice has been made to reject God's help. **Truth#68: Through a lifestyle of repentance, the saint acknowledges his character flaws as he judges his smitten heart of its foolhardiness!**

The Catered Heart

In chapter 24 verses 16-24, we learn that repentance must cost something. **Truth #69: Merely, stating "I repent" or to follow the instructions from a pulpit without a cost factor involved negates true, godly repentance, because it is evangelical, in scope. However, through a lifestyle of repentance, the saint makes provision for the renewal of the spirit of his mind and the regeneration of his soul, by taking special pain to cater his heart to God!** As Joel 2:13 states, *"...rend your heart and not your garments..."* The saint of God must allow the Spirit of God to work His goodness into the deepest recesses of his character [heart]. Otherwise, the saint wastes his time. **Truth #70: All commitments to a lifestyle of repentance involves our mutual participation, because repentance activates the atoning power found in the blood!** *(cf. Lev. 23:27-29; Rom. 12:1-3)*

Notes:

Chapter 12
Repentance in the Book of 1ˢᵗ Kings

1 Kings 8:44-49
"If thy people go out to battle against their enemy, whithersoever thou shalt send them, and shalt pray unto the Lord toward the city which thou hast chosen, and toward the house that I have built for thy name: Then hear thou in heaven their prayer and their supplication, and **maintain their cause***. If they sin against thee, (for there is no man that sinneth not), and thou be angry with them, and deliver them to the enemy, so that they carry them away captives unto the land of the enemy, far or near, Yet if they shall bethink themselves in the land whither they were carried captives, and* **repent***, and make supplication unto thee in the land of them that carried them captives, saying, We have sinned, and have done perversely, we have committed wickedness. And so return unto thee with all their heart, and with all their soul, in the land of their enemies, ...then hear thou their prayers and their supplication in heaven thy dwelling place, and* **maintain their cause***."* (emphasis mine)

In League with Our Lobbyist

There must be a cause bigger and greater than the saint of God to bring him to a point of supplication. Consider the lobbyist. Big money is paid to the lobbyist and he in turn, represents his constituents as he brings their issues to the governing body. There, the lobbyist maintains their cause! Since money was exchanged between the lobbyist and his constituents, the lobbyist speaks up for and on the behalf of his sponsorship. **Truth #71: Repentance then is recognizing Jesus Christ as the lobbyist, who paid His own price to maintain our cause!** Therefore, the saint must agree with God, and be in league with Him for his cause, based upon His Word! As lobbyist, Jesus Christ is also our Mediator Who stands in proxy for us. *(cf. 2 Chron. 6:37-39; Heb. 8:6; 12:24; 1 John 2:1)*

Presumption Negates Repentance

Truth # 72: A lifestyle of repentance then is a cause and a pursuit of a mission in and throughout life. Repentance is a cause for battle, and as an entreaty, this lifestyle calls upon God to maintain our cause. Repentance gives strength for the battle, because repentance is an assurance of victory and strength for the battles of life! *(cf. 1 Kgs. 8:44-45)* Too many presume that true repentance before God is based solely upon a rebirth experience, if in fact there ever was one. Misunderstanding repentance prevents the saint from working out his salvation with fear and trembling. *(cf. Phil. 2:12)* God is not playing patty cake! And yet, too many in the church are! *(cf. 1 Kgs. 20:18)*

Chapter 13

Repentance in the Book of 2nd Kings

Talk About Going to Hell in a Hand Basket
2 Kings 17:12-14
"For they served idols, whereof the Lord had said unto them, Ye shall not do this thing. Yet the Lord testified against Israel, and against Judah, by all the prophets, and by all the seers, saying, Turn ye from your evil ways, and keep my commandments and my statutes, according to all the law which I commanded your fathers, and which I sent to you, by my servants the prophets. Notwithstanding, **they would not hear, but hardened their necks,** *like to the neck of their fathers, that did not believe in the Lord their God."* (emphasis mine)

As a nation, the Israelis sinned against God through idolatry. The rest of the chapter describes the abominable conditions of their corruption and their wickedness. It's as if total anarchy existed, because of a mob psychology which was probably, "Well, since everyone else is doing it, it must be alright!" No doubt that this rebellion was permitted to develop, because of the corrupt leadership who oppressed the people. Since when does a mob mentality accomplish anything other than lawlessness and confusion? We see this in America and throughout the world even today! In the verses above, Almighty God pleaded with the people to turn from their idolatries, but they refused. Now, this is an illustration of going to hell in a hand basket!

The Church that is Defined by Faith and Repentance

Desperate situations often require harsh remedies! An impasse existed between the Israelis and Almighty God! The situation was deadlocked! Something had to be done to thwart this rebellion. There was no avoiding it and there was no escape. This contention seemed to possess no diplomatic solution. Almighty God had a good argument against the people, but the people had a controversy with God! Sounds like the picture of the traditional church today, doesn't it? Although they may be myriad, God's methods are immutable. What He did then, He shall accomplish again. In this eleventh hour of man's history, God has sent His prophets [preachers of righteousness] to the many denominational churches of this church age, exhorting them towards repentance. Since the leadership of these churches have long since replaced the Word of God with their denominational dogma, by default, they allowed the New Testament Church to evolve into denominationalism! It must be remembered that The New Testament Church is defined by faith and repentance, and not by denominationalism! The denominational church, although once established in faith and repentance have, over the decades and centuries, evolved into institutions which are based upon the traditions of men. These are meager attempts to structure, orchestrate and control the basic elements of God's Word! Not to mention that denominational churches have taken advantage of the Name of Jesus Christ for their own gain! Therefore, what evolution is to creation, denominationalism is to the commandments of God! *(Mk. 7:6-9)*

The Line of Righteous Judgment

2 Kings 21:13
"And I will stretch over Jerusalem the measuring line of Samaria and the plummet of the house of Ahab; and I will wipe Jerusalem as one wipes a dish, wiping it and turning it upside down."

The judgment of God shall be levied against all those who resemble or imitate others in their sins. These copy cats must expect to receive the same fare as they with whom they are in league with. Whereas, Jesus Christ is the Alpha and the Omega to the righteous, selfishness has become the beginning and the conclusion of all the miseries which carnality provides to the unrighteous! The illustration of dish washing is meant to infer that all wickedness shall be purged and that no such thing shall enter heaven. First, there is the scrubbing and then there is the rinsing of that which has been scrubbed. *(cf. Eph. 5:27; 2Pet. 3:14)*

Repentance Brings Restoration

In chapter 22, we read of the rediscovery of the "book of the law." It was found in the house of the Lord and not in some other institution! The interesting thing here is that when just wages and monies were finally and rightly assessed to the workers in the house of God, then the book was found. The import being, that when the church rightly assesses herself, with a faith quality decision to do justly, through a lifestyle of repentance, God will allow His book to be rediscovered. **Truth #73: Through a lifestyle of repentance, the saint will no longer compartmentalize his relationship with God, separating or excluding the workings of God's righteousness from his daily living!** Rather, the saint will embrace the precious Holy Spirit in every facet of his livelihood. **Truth #74: Through a lifestyle of repentance, the saint offers a just wage as a spiritual judgment against his carnality!** A tender heart resigns itself of the carnality within, for this resignation is a byproduct of a lifestyle of repentance. This resolution, as a heart felt purpose, will provoke a display of outrage with utter disgust and despair for all the abominations of society, so much so, that even the tearing away of that which is material and of weeping will be evident. This conduct of contrition will most definitely get God's attention!

Coming Summer/2015

...the investigation continues.
This is 2nd Book in the incredible FREEDOM SERIES

One of the keys to turning this once great Nation around is turning back to God. WE TURN AROUND - REPENT. Ed Marr breaks this subject down into easy to understand, bite-sized nuggets of Truth, that will help Anyone, any Church, any Government and any Nation SHINE AGAIN!

Available at select Bookstores and
www.boldtruthpublishing.com

JUST RELEASED!
A NEW Song Single on CD
by Author & Prophetic Teacher Ed Marr

Direct from God's Heart to Yours "*Receive My Love*" is an open invitation for intimate fellowship from The Father to a lost and hurting America.

"The overwhelming sense of God's never-ending love for humanity comes through loud and clear. The inspired lyrics mixed with one of my favorite tunes, made me smile down on the inside."
— Aaron Jones, Missionary

Available at select Bookstores and
www.boldtruthpublishing.com

Check out these other Great Books from BOLD TRUTH PUBLISHING

by Adrienne Gottlieb

• ISRAEL'S LEGITIMACY
Why We Should Protect Israel At All Cost

• The Replacement Theology LIE
The Book Jews wished every Christian would read

-----

by Daryl Holloman

• Seemed Good to The Holy Ghost
Inspired Teachings by Brother Daryl
PLUS - Prophecies spoken in Pardo, Cebu, Philippines

• The Adventures of Hezekiah Hare & Ernie Byrd
A Children's Bible Adventure

• Further Adventures
More Good News as Hezekiah & Ernie follow Jesus.

-----

by Steve Young

• SIX FEET DEEP
Burying Your Past with Forgiveness

-----

by Paul Howard

• THE FAITH WALK
Keys to walking in VICTORY!

------

by Joe Waggnor

• Bless THE KING
Praise Poems for My Lord and Saviour

by Jerry W. Hollenbeck
• The KINGDOM of GOD
An Agrarian Society
*Featuring The Kingdom Realities, Bible Study Course,
Research and Development Classes*

• The Word of God
FATHER • WORD • SPIRIT
Literally THE WORD

-----

by Ed Marr
• C. H. P.
Coffee Has Priority
The Memoirs of a California Highway Patrol - Badge 9045

----

by Mary Ann England
• Women in Ministry
*From her Teachings at the FCF Bible School - Tulsa, Oklahoma
(Foreword by Pat Harrison)*

----

by James Jonsten
• WHO is GOD to YOU?
The path to know the most misunderstood name in the universe.

------

by Aaron Jones
• In the SECRET PLACE of THE MOST HIGH
God's Word for Supernatural Healing, Deliverance and Protection

• SOUND from HEAVEN
Praying in Tongues for a Victorious Life

See more Books and all of our products at
www.BoldTruthPublishing.com

A MUST READ

Powerful testimony of what God did in, to, and through one State Traffic Officer.

"Action-packed, an intriguing mix of lawful AUTHORITY and Holy Ghost POWER. I thoroughly enjoyed it!"

- Pastor Kenn Watson
VICTORY Assembly of God

Available at select Bookstores and
www.boldtruthpublishing.com

www.ingramcontent.com/pod-product-compliance
Lightning Source LLC
Chambersburg PA
CBHW070756100426
42742CB00012B/2160